Little Laureates 2008

Yorkshire
Edited by Angela Fairbrace

Young Writers

First published in Great Britain in 2008 by:
Young Writers
Remus House
Coltsfoot Drive
Peterborough
PE2 9JX
Telephone: 01733 890066
Website: www.youngwriters.co.uk

All Rights Reserved

© *Copyright Contributors 2008*

SB ISBN 978-1 84431 603 2

Foreword

Young Writers was established in 1991 and has been passionately devoted to the promotion of reading and writing in children and young adults ever since. The quest continues today. Young Writers remains as committed to the nurturing of poetic and literary talent as ever.

This year's Young Writers competition has proven as vibrant and dynamic as ever and we are delighted to present a showcase of the best poetry from across the UK and in some cases overseas. Each poem has been selected from a wealth of *Little Laureates 2008* entries before ultimately being published in this, our seventeenth primary school poetry series.

Once again, we have been supremely impressed by the overall quality of the entries we have received. The imagination, energy and creativity which has gone into each young writer's entry made choosing the poems a challenging and often difficult but ultimately hugely rewarding task - the general high standard of the work submitted ensured this opportunity to bring their poetry to a larger appreciative audience.

We sincerely hope you are pleased with this final collection and that you will enjoy *Little Laureates 2008 Yorkshire* for many years to come.

Contents

Beck Primary School, Sheffield
    Kian Cooper (8)   1

Christ Church Upper Armley CE Primary School, Leeds
    Charlotte Louise Wade (9)   1
    Lauren Lydon (10)   1
    Jasmine Parmar (10)   2
    Timothy Parker (9)   3
    Flora Jane Thomas (9)   3
    Matthew Hirst (10)   4
    Kyle Drayton (10)   4
    Ibrahim Hussain & Lewis Logan (10)   5
    Kieron Lister (9)   5
    Toni Ann Hawke (9)   6
    Luke Johnson & Aidan McGonigle (10)   6
    Rosie Mai Clough (10)   7
    Kieron Palmer (10)   7

Cundall Manor School, York
    Charlotte Saxby (8)   8
    Cy Worthington (9)   8
    Nathan Hale (8)   8
    Edward Bottomley (8)   9
    Toby Caulfield (8)   9
    Josh Hall (8)   9
    Alice Foster (8)   10
    James Green (9)   10
    Antony Hunzinger (9)   10
    Sophie Helfferich (8)   11
    Joseph Keegan (8)   11
    Quentin England (8)   11
    Erin Porter (8)   12
    Harry Whitworth (8)   12
    Charlotte Hoggan (8)   12
    India Clements (8)   13
    Lauren Egan (8)   13
    Verity Pern (8)   13
    James Gordon (8)   14
    Thomas Wood (8)   14

Dorchester Primary School, Hull
Christopher McKenzie (10)	14
Kieran Spencer (9)	15
Shaquille Bayles (9)	15
Alex Burdick (9)	16
Danielle Hughes (9)	16

Holywell Green Primary School, Halifax
Bethany Wilkinson (9)	17
Chloe Firth (9)	17
Abigail Langton (11)	18
Jessica White-Travis (10)	19
Teri-Ann Watson (10)	20
Jack Raby (10)	20
Paisley Macarthur (10)	21
Matthew Ramsden (10)	21
Jacy Ellis (9)	22
Katie Wilson (9)	22
Rachel Smith (10)	23
Jordan Bowers (10)	23
Beth Ashton-Robson (10)	24
Joshua Gleadell (10)	24
Daniel Smith (10)	25
Jessica Smith (10)	25
April Willows (10)	26
Jack Brudenell (11)	26
Haydn Corns (10)	26
Michael Silvester (9)	27
Jordan Thompson (9)	27

Longman's Hill CP School, Selby
Ellie Rafton (9)	27
Lucy Crawford (10)	28
Bethany Watson (11)	28
Erin Clark (11)	29
Jack Barker (10)	29
Oliver Bloxham (11)	30
Jake Douglas (10)	30
Jessica Young (11)	31
Liam Foster (11)	31
Georgia Southern (11)	32

Ben Moate (11)	32
Kayleigh Richardson (10)	33
Rhianna MacDonald (10)	33
Harvey Rodgers (11)	34
Sam Ness (10)	34
Olivia Scott (10)	35
Scott Wilson (10)	35
Anna Barrett (9)	36
Courtney Chambers (9)	37
Mark Taylor (9)	38

Northstead CP School, Scarborough

Ben Foster (11)	38
Luke Sutcliffe (10)	39
Jacob Hird (10)	39
Alaina Chambers (11)	40
Catherine Hutchinson (10)	40
Zachary Slater (10)	41
Roxanne Cusworth (10)	41
Ashleigh Pratt (10)	42
Sharna Cooper (10)	42
Thomas McNally (11)	43
Tyler Chapman (11)	43
William Gibson (10)	44
James Deaves (10)	44
Jacob Stocks (10)	45
Sophie Dent (10)	45
Thomas Brace (11)	46
Abigale Craig (11)	46
Hayley Towell (10)	47
Lucy Hirstle (11)	47

Ravensworth CE Primary School, Richmond

Toni Hutchinson & Ellie Blenkiron (11)	48
Ruth Bernard & Molly Maddison (9)	48
Chloe Barrett (11)	49
Abby Metcalfe (10)	49
Alexander James Lillie (9)	50
Ben Tennant & Will Turnbull (10)	50
Victoria Marcelino-Purse (10)	50
Bethaney Rush (10)	51

Lauren Kemp (10)	51
Rachel Stirr (11)	51
Chloé Burrows (10)	52
Adam Wallis (10)	52

St Joseph's RC Primary School, Doncaster
Mackenzie Charlesworth (8)	52

St Joseph's Primary School, Pontefract
Daniel McDonnell (10)	53
Callum Hughes (10)	53
Ben Booth (10)	53
Helen Walsh (10)	54
Joseph Paul Taylor (10)	54
Natalya Wilson (10)	54

Sandringham Primary School, Doncaster
Tyler Wright (10)	55
Shannon Smith (11)	55
Edward Miles (11)	56
Helen Wilson (10)	56
Connor Martin (10)	57
Charlotte Nesbitt (11)	57
Paige Williams (11)	58
Georgia Morton (11)	58
Liam Davies (11)	59
Jake Lockwood (11)	59
Ryan Ellis (10)	60
Bethany Atkinson (11)	60
Lucy Davison (10)	61
Diben Pun (11)	61
Rebecca Thirlwell (11)	62
Adam Kean (11)	62
Aisha Miller (11)	63
Bradley Maltby (10)	63
Jordan Quinn (10)	64
Dominik Tylicki (10)	64
Liam Simmons (10)	65
Matthew Jewell (10)	65
Rebecca Wynne (10)	66
Caitlin Bower (10)	66

Bethany Alton (11)   67
Shelby Amess (10)   67
Jack Burton (10)   68
Jordan Jackson (10)   68
Kelly Baxendale (10)   69
Matthew Jones (11)   69
Phoebe Grantham (10)   70

South Cave CE Primary School, Brough
Beth MacDonald (8)   70
Sophie James (8)   71
Ellis Teal (9)   71
Lacko Karsai (9)   72
Molly Horsfield (8)   72
Lucy Lowther (9)   73
Dean Makowski-Clayton (8)   73
Lucy Reast (9)   74
Harvey Plows (8)   74
Ruth Dobson (8)   75
Finlay Hills (8)   75
Madeleine Borman (8)   76
Hannah Ozsanlav (8)   76
Aimee Olsson (9)   77
Hollie Ferguson-Pratt (8)   77
William Joseph Branagan (8)   78
George Thornham (8)   78
Shannon O'Loughlin (8)   79
Tom Watson (9)   79
Elizabeth Haigh   80
Jack Henderson (9)   80
Eleanor Raitt (9)   81
Louis Stevenson (8)   81
Georgia Eve Smith (8)   82
Emma Williamson (8)   83
Kristian White (8)   83
Joshua Moore (8)   84
Jade Smith (9)   84
Chloe Hiles (9)   85
Tobias Pometsey (8)   85
Ben Sage (8)   86
Fay Inverarity (8)   86

Oliver Drake (9) — 86
Sam Moment (8) — 87
James Finlay (9) — 87

Southcoates Primary School, Hull
Aidan Forrester (8) — 87
Reece Brewitt (8) — 88
Joshua Cain (8) — 88
Abigail Rose Betts (11) — 88
Jack Brown (7) — 89
Toby Hazel (9) — 89
Toni Andrews (7) — 89
Chelsey Robinson (8) — 90
Shanice Bell (7) — 90
Luke Christensen (9) — 90
Jessica Morgan (8) — 91
Cane Donkin (9) — 91
Megan Seaton (8) — 91
Chloe Jackson (8) — 92
Elliott Hepworth (10) — 92
Kieron Cawkwell (10) — 92
Lauren Leigh Allison-Beedle (10) — 93
Lara Osborne (10) — 93
Sasha Gabriel (11) — 93
Kellie Adamson (10) — 94
Deanna May Hughes (10) — 94
Ellie-May Betts (8) — 94
Ellie Winstanley (7) — 95
Amy Watkin (8) — 95
Tiffany Gabriel (8) — 95
Jordan Bartley (8) — 96
Lucy Betts (8) — 96
Libbie Thompson (8) — 96
Jessica Wilkinson (8) — 97
Kallum Robins (8) — 97
Amy Kirkwood (8) — 97
Sophie Walker (8) — 98
Alice Watkin (8) — 98
Jack Walsh (7) — 98
Sophie Arnold (8) — 99

Callum Barton (8) — 99
Courtney Young (8) — 99
Joshua Martin (9) — 100
Cameron Cook (9) — 100
Lee Bonner (10) — 100
Charlotte Blackburn (10) — 101
Ellie Kerins (11) — 101
Sean Boddy (11) — 101
Lucy Edwards (9) — 102
Reece Cockerline (11) — 102
Scott Baker (9) — 103
Reece Stewart (10) — 103
Jason Weightman (10) — 104
Jakob Sheffield (10) — 104
Rosie Plews (10) — 105
Andrew Wallace (10) — 105
Charles Weaver (9) — 106
Shannan Warelow (10) — 106
Chloe Snell (10) — 107
Scott Thornley (11) — 107
Selina Johnson (11) — 108
Amy Brown (11) — 108
Shauna Denman (10) — 109
Charley Hornshaw (10) — 109
Charlie Bailey (10) — 110
Rona Carmena Spiteri (10) — 110
Maisie Hopkin (9) — 111

Spring Cottage Primary School, Hull

Louis Dearing (8) — 111
Shelby Swaby (9) — 112
George Thompson (9) — 113
Natasha Richardson (8) — 114
Sarah Jordan (8) — 115
Emma Hewison (8) — 116
Ryan Rhoades (8) — 117
Sophie Louise Maw (8) — 118
Jack Edward Dawson (9) — 119
Eleanor Tyas (9) — 120
Lloyd Gurnell (9) — 121

Courtney Rose Meakes (8) 122
Ashleigh Dixon 123
Ellie Johnson (8) 124

The Poems

The Garden

Poisonous pond pretends to be pretty.
Flying flowers flip into the air.
Shattering shed shows a shoe what to do.
Tremendous tree tosses coins all day.
Cruel grass phones the cops.

Kian Cooper (8)
Beck Primary School, Sheffield

Gingerbread Man

Gingerbread men can be different sizes,
Different colours, different clothes,
They sometimes like to pose,
In their best made clothes.

They taste like ginger in the sun,
They look like a burnt sun,
They smell like burnt wood,
They are *gorgeous!*

Charlotte Louise Wade (9)
Christ Church Upper Armley CE Primary School, Leeds

My Brothers

My brothers are a pain in the back
They play with sacks
They lie on mats
They always do SATs
They are scared of bats.

Lauren Lydon (10)
Christ Church Upper Armley CE Primary School, Leeds

Seasons

Spring is here
Flowers at your door
And then some more.
There's a blue sky all clear
With not a single smear
Love is in the air
Valentine's Day is near
Then there's Easter
But it's over now
A new season is here.

Summer is here
The sun is out
And we all shout.
Fun and joy
As we play with our new toy
Busy bees
Going in trees
But it's over now
A new season's here.

Autumn is here
Bright, colourful lights in the air
Glowing in the dark night sky.
Who's that knocking at your door?
Fear in your eyes
As you open the door to a great big surprise
But it's over now
A new season is here!

Winter is here
The snow is falling
People are calling
Christmas is almost here
So is the New Year
But it's over now
It's the end of the year.

Jasmine Parmar (10)
Christ Church Upper Armley CE Primary School, Leeds

Sugar Food

Apples with toffee on for Andrew
Bubblegum of all flavours for Bert
Cake for Charlotte
Double Decker for David
Every kind of pop for Eric
Frazzels for Fred
Galaxy bar for Georgia
Help, the kids are getting too fat!
Ice cream for Ibi
Jaffa cakes for Jordan
King-sized Calipo ice cream for Kieron
Liquorice for Lewis
Minstrels for Matthew
NikNaks for Neil
Orange sweets for Olivia
Parma violets for Paul
Quavers for the Queen
Revels for Rosie
Someone having Slush Puppie
Tiger bars for Tim
White chocolate for William
Xotic fruit juice
Yellow sweets all for Yasmin
Zac starts it all over again.

Timothy Parker (9)
Christ Church Upper Armley CE Primary School, Leeds

Hard Work

I hate hard work
I work on Monday
I work on Tuesday
I work on Wednesday
I work on Thursday
I work on Friday
Work, work, boring work!

Flora Jane Thomas (9)
Christ Church Upper Armley CE Primary School, Leeds

Holidays

The time of year for having fun,
Spending time in the sun.
Time off school,
Splashing in the pool.
Holidays, holidays are the best.

The sand is hot and gold,
The sea is blue and cold.
All the sandcastles are handmade,
Built with a bucket and spade.
Holidays, holidays are the best.

The ice cream is so big,
We spill them while we play tig.
Shorts, suncream and hats,
We arrive at the beach and lay out our mats.
Holidays, holidays are the best.

Matthew Hirst (10)
Christ Church Upper Armley CE Primary School, Leeds

Rugby

I like rugby
It is fun
I play with my friends
Out in the sun.

I like rugby
It is tough
We play with a rugby ball
We are rough.

Kyle Drayton (10)
Christ Church Upper Armley CE Primary School, Leeds

Everything Funny

Funny friends:
Funny friends are so funny,
They look like a bunny
And they like honey
And they sunbathe when it's sunny.

Funny monkeys:
Funny monkeys swing from vines,
Funny monkeys draw lines,
Funny monkeys have wobbly spines,
Funny monkeys play with pines.

Funny monsters:
Funny monsters give you a scare,
Funny monsters give you a tear,
Funny monsters eat pears,
Funny monsters fight with a bear.

Ibrahim Hussain & Lewis Logan (10)
Christ Church Upper Armley CE Primary School, Leeds

Wind

Wind, wind blows you away
Blows you here
Blows you there
Blows you everywhere.

It rocks the trees
It vibrates the bars
Breaks your aerial
How annoying!

Kieron Lister (9)
Christ Church Upper Armley CE Primary School, Leeds

My Bedroom

My bedroom is a mess,
What can I say?
It is my new bedroom,
I got it on New Year's Day.
My dad is going crazy,
Pulling out his hair,

I've blamed my little sister,
I tell him every day.
My bedroom is a mess,
I don't know what to do,
I think I'll have to tidy up,
It's the only thing to do.

Toni Ann Hawke (9)
Christ Church Upper Armley CE Primary School, Leeds

Wild At Heart

Lions roar
Some animals are carnivores
Hyenas go *ha, ha*
Chimpanzees go *la, la*
Tigers are vicious
Meat is delicious
Bats flap
Hunters set traps
Cheetahs are fast
Animals live till their last
Animals go hyper
Hunters have a sniper.

Luke Johnson & Aidan McGonigle (10)
Christ Church Upper Armley CE Primary School, Leeds

My Dog, Georgia

My dog is so cute,
My dog is so playful,
My dog is so loving
And makes me so cheerful.

She is so active
And so happy too,
If you walk through the door,
She jumps on top of you.

She loves me so much
And my brother and sister as well,
When she walks her collar jingles,
Just like a jingle bell.

Rosie Mai Clough (10)
Christ Church Upper Armley CE Primary School, Leeds

Water, Water, Stay Away

Water, water,
You are so boring
You are back
And you don't help people.
So water, water,
Stay away.
Police help people,
They need boots,
People didn't survive.

Kieron Palmer (10)
Christ Church Upper Armley CE Primary School, Leeds

The Moon

The moon is a silver spoon neatly laid on a black tablecloth
It is a freshly picked daisy on a lady's black morning hat
It is a lily petal floating on a dark pool
It is a white lid from a water bottle
It is a white football kicked high into the night sky
It is a white bit of chalk on some black paper
It is a silver medal on a dark fleece
The moon is the queen of the night.

Charlotte Saxby (8)
Cundall Manor School, York

What Is Pink?

Pink is the strawberry milkshake
That I drink every day,
Pink is the stripe on a bowling ball,
That I bowl my own way.
Pink is a pretty tulip,
Sprayed with a garden hose,
Pink is the colour of the sunset,
But eventually it goes.
I think pink is the best of all!

Cy Worthington (9)
Cundall Manor School, York

Hedgehogs - Haiku

Hedgehogs are so cute
They hibernate in the fall
They are very small.

Nathan Hale (8)
Cundall Manor School, York

What Is Red?

Red is the colour of a van delivering post
Red is the colour of fire at night
Red is the colour of a dog winning a show
Red is the colour of house lights sparkling at night
Red is the colour of a postbox shining on a summer's day
Red is the colour of a football team, maybe winning a game.

Edward Bottomley (8)
Cundall Manor School, York

What Is Brown?

Brown is the colour of a playful Bengal kitten
Brown is the colour of soft soil
Brown is the colour of yummy chocolate
Brown is the colour of fresh baked bread
Brown is the colour of beautiful leaves in the autumn
Brown is the colour of the amazing bark on the trees
Brown is the king of nature.

Toby Caulfield (8)
Cundall Manor School, York

The Sun

The sun is an orange Tic Tac in your mouth.
The sun is a bumblebee collecting yummy honey.
The sun is a yellow fish oil waiting for some water.
The sun is the light bulb of the day.

Josh Hall (8)
Cundall Manor School, York

Red

Red is a rose freshly picked from a lovely garden.
Red is the colour of my mum's lipstick when she goes out.
Red is the colour of the sunset, it is a beautiful pinkish colour.
Red is the colour of a red dragonfly which has landed on a pretty
blue pond.
Red is the colour of a blazing fire which has just been lit.
Red is the colour of a poppy on Remembrance Day.
Red is the queen of all colours.

Alice Foster (8)
Cundall Manor School, York

The Sun

A nice juicy peach with some nectarine
A giant, juicy orange sitting on the tree
The sun is a lovely golden apple waiting on a bright blue plate to
be eaten
The bright blue plate is shining, it's too hot for me.

James Green (9)
Cundall Manor School, York

Blue

Blue is the colour of waves crashing and storming through the sea
Blue is the colour of bluebells lighting up the world
Blue is the colour of the sky that makes my eyes twinkle and shine
Blue is truly the best colour of them all.

Antony Hunzinger (9)
Cundall Manor School, York

What Is Yellow?

Yellow is a smiley banana from a fresh farm.
Yellow is a shimmering, glimmering yellow car just come out of a
car wash.
Yellow is a duck swimming in a deep blue pond.
Bright yellow sunset on blue sky with jet-black birds flying around it.
Swirls of yummy, golden custard on inky blueberries.

Sophie Helfferich (8)
Cundall Manor School, York

The Moon

The moon is a glowing, shiny beetle glaring at you.
The moon is a rotten apple shining in the deep black sky.
The moon is a beautiful, big crystal flying in the sky.
The moon is a giant, white football floating in the sky.
The moon is a big banana in the black sky.
The moon is the queen of the darkness.

Joseph Keegan (8)
Cundall Manor School, York

What Is Orange?

Orange can be the sun, bright on a summer's day.
Orange is a big smelly flower swishing in the wind.
Orange can be blazing, scorching fire burning through the day.
Orange can be a juicy, scrumptious peach sitting on a plate.
Orange is the most famous colour of all.

Quentin England (8)
Cundall Manor School, York

The Moon

The moon is a diamond on a velvet hankie
It is a fresh daisy falling on the dark blue sea
My friend thinks the moon is a sparkling sticker
On a dark blue piece of paper
My teacher thinks it is a fresh tissue
On a black envelope
But I think the moon is the queen of the night sky
Falling down a dark blue slide.

Erin Porter (8)
Cundall Manor School, York

The Moon

The moon is a shiny silver metal,
It flies in the midnight sky.
The moon is a bright white goblet,
Next to the dark blue sky.
The moon is a bright white torch,
In the dark blue sea.
The moon is the queen of the night.

Harry Whitworth (8)
Cundall Manor School, York

Butterflies - Haiku

Butterflies fly high
In the great, bright, sunny sky
The best flying things!

Charlotte Hoggan (8)
Cundall Manor School, York

The Moon

The moon is a silver sixpence on a black cloak in the darkness.
I think the moon is a fresh daisy growing on a velvet cat.
The moon is a big, fabulous silver spoon lying on a bright football.
The moon is a gorgeous diamond flying in the sky.
The moon is the queen of the night.

India Clements (8)
Cundall Manor School, York

The Sun

It is a glowing spider that has only just been born.
It is a brand new golden coin magically coming up calmly.
It is like a red thumb print on light blue paper.
It warms the Earth in the morning, making its way across the calm sea.
The sun is the queen through the day, like a yellow crystal pool
                                                                                of water.

Lauren Egan (8)
Cundall Manor School, York

The Moon

The moon is a silver swan,
It swims in black night water and glows every night.
The moon is a shimmering silver spoon,
Lying on a dark blue cloth.
It is a bumpy rock,
On a blue sand bed.
But honestly, I think the moon is the king of the night sky.

Verity Pern (8)
Cundall Manor School, York

What Is Red?

Red is the colour of the blazing sunset
Red is the colour of the postbox
It is the light of the fire
But most of all, it's the team *I desire*.

James Gordon (8)
Cundall Manor School, York

Haikus

Lollipops:
I like lollipops
I collect them in a jar
Strawberry's the best.

Dotty:
Dotty is my dog
She is fourteen years of age
I love her so much.

Thomas Wood (8)
Cundall Manor School, York

Hate

Hate is like blood
The sound is a little girl
Screaming for life!

The taste is like
Dark poison
The smell is gunpowder
Going off.

The look is like a pile of dark mud
It really reminds me of
Ashes in the wind.

Christopher McKenzie (10)
Dorchester Primary School, Hull

Love

Love is red
For the colour of hearts
Love is the colour
Of the daffodils in my garden

Love sounds like people
Kissing in the background
Love sounds like
Breath of other people

Love tastes like
Sugary and sweet
Love tastes like
Vanilla ice cream and mints

Love reminds you of
Other people
Like your family, your friends, pets
Roses and daffodils.

Kieran Spencer (9)
Dorchester Primary School, Hull

Hate

Hate is red
Like the blood of your fingers
Hate sounds like
A girl screaming
As loud as she can
It tastes like sick
Running down your chin.

Hate smells like gunpowder
It looks like half man, half beast
Hate reminds me of a volcano erupting
And dead bodies in a coffin.

Shaquille Bayles (9)
Dorchester Primary School, Hull

Please Mrs Kay
(Inspired by 'Please Mrs Butler' by Alan Ahlberg)

'Please Mrs Kay
This boy Darren Snow
Keeps getting my pencil, Miss
Where can I go?'

'Go out the door
Now go to your next class
Go and sit on the floor
With the hall pass.'

'Please Mrs Kay
This boy Darren Snow
Keeps poking me, Miss
Where can I go?'

'Go get a ball
Go to the sea
Go catch a fish
But don't ask me!'

Alex Burdick (9)
Dorchester Primary School, Hull

Please Miss Kay
(Inspired by 'Please Mrs Butler' by Alan Ahlberg)

'Please Miss Kay
This girl, Chloe Snow
Keeps giving me mucky looks, Miss
Where shall I go?'

'Please Miss Kay
This girl, Chloe Snow
Keeps eating my cheese, Miss
Where shall I go?'

'Go and sit in the hall, dear
Hide behind a tree
Do whatever you can, my sweet
But don't ask me!'

Danielle Hughes (9)
Dorchester Primary School, Hull

Monkeys

Forwards, backwards, up and down,
A monkey's movement will make you frown.

Hairy, fluffy, rough and freaky,
Unusual monkeys are very creepy.
Banana eater, tree lover,
Small, brown, a brilliant hugger.

Forwards, backwards, up and down,
A monkey's movement will make you frown

Better than teddies, soft as a feather,
And even better than sunny weather.
So I'm glad that monkeys are alive,
I wish I was one, then I could go on tree rides.

Forwards, backwards, up and down,
A monkey's movement will make you frown.

Bethany Wilkinson (9)
Holywell Green Primary School, Halifax

A Tree Frog

A ngry, red, fiery feet

T ouch its skin, very squishy
R ubbery, bright animal, but very cute
E ffective creature with delicate legs
E legant, bouncing onto strange plants

F rogs leaping from tree to tree
R ough, slimy skin, shiny as can be
O range, red eyes, bumpy, weird head
G reen, wet feet, multicoloured arms.

Chloe Firth (9)
Holywell Green Primary School, Halifax

The Jabberhockey
(Based on 'Jabberwocky' by Lewis Carroll)

'Twas Friday and the hockey players
Did gyre and gimble in the rink,
All mimsy were the Borogrove fans
And Mr Rath was rather pink.

'Beware the Jabberhockeys, my team!
Their blades that bite, their sticks that catch,
Beware the coach bird, and shun
The point-scoring snatch.'

They took their L-shaped sticks in hand,
Long time of the endless lose they sought,
So rested them while half-time began
And sat a while in thought.

And as if in huffish thought they sat,
The Jabberhockey with eyes of flame,
Came charging through the ice rink doors
And scowled as they came!

One, two, three, four and more and more,
The Borogroves went snicker-snack,
They lost again, but not in vain,
Their lost hearts went black.

'And hast thou lost again, my lads?
Come to my training club for boys!'
'Oh, fabulous day, wahoo, wahey!'
They chortled in their joy.

'Twas Friday and the hockey players,
Did gyre and gimble in the rink,
All mimsy were the Borogrove fans
And Mr Rath was rather pink.

Abigail Langton (11)
Holywell Green Primary School, Halifax

Anteater

Anteater, very slow, time to eat, off he goes.
Ants on logs, what a treat,
Better than human flesh or meat.
Even though he's a furry thing,
His ants greet him like a king.

Round ears, shiny nose,
Longer than the longest hose.

Human coming, what to do?
Human hunter coming for you.
Anteater petrified, what will he be,
Stewed or fried?

Round ears, shiny nose,
Longer than the longest hose.

Arrow ready, aim, *fire!*
Anteater jumps a little higher.
Net above and trapdoor,
Anteater's life is no more.

Round ears, shiny nose,
Longer than the longest hose.

One ant left, just enough,
To make the anteater nice and tough.
He jumped up ready to pounce,
Even though he weighs one ounce.
Red eyes glare at the man,
He ran away, what a very nice day.

Round ears, shiny nose,
Longer than the longest hose.

Jessica White-Travis (10)
Holywell Green Primary School, Halifax

Children
(Inspired by 'Ten Little Schoolboys' by A A Milne)

Ten mischievous children playing in the sand,
One saw their dad and then there were nine.

Nine mischievous children messing up the school,
One saw some chocolate and then there were eight.

Eight mischievous children eating their dinner,
One saw the fish tank and then there were seven.

Seven mischievous children having a nap,
One had a nightmare and then there were six.

Six mischievous children playing with their toys,
One went to the toilet and then there were five.

Five mischievous children fighting with each other,
One got hurt and then there were four.

Four mischievous children jumping up and down,
One fell over and then there were three.

Three mischievous children in the bath,
One got out, so then there were two.

Two mischievous children sitting in the yard,
One went home and then there was one.

One lonely child thinking of something to do,
One went for a wander and then there was none.

Teri-Ann Watson (10)
Holywell Green Primary School, Halifax

Haiku

What a goal for Crouch
It's 2-1 to Liverpool
And Liverpool win.

Jack Raby (10)
Holywell Green Primary School, Halifax

Mums
(Inspired by 'Ten Little Schoolboys' by A A Milne)

Ten mums standing in a line,
One saw a Thorntons shop and then there were nine.
Nine mums standing by the school gate,
One saw a puppy and then there were eight.
Eight mums on a plane to Devon,
One saw a Galaxy bar and then there were seven.
Seven mums eating a Twix,
One saw a 50% off every two yoghurts and then there were six
Six mums sunbathing in the park,
One saw a beehive and then there were five.
Five mums in a fight,
One fell into the door and then there were four.
Four mums having a cup of tea,
One threw up and then there were three.
Three mums in the pub,
One had to change a nappy full of poo and then there were two.
Two mums were angry because they got conned,
One went off crying and then there was one.
One mum all alone,
She said, 'I might as well go home,' and then there was none.

Paisley Macarthur (10)
Holywell Green Primary School, Halifax

Roller Coaster Horror

So excited, can't wait
Thrilling at the top
Oh my God!
Oh no!
Again!
Wooo!

Matthew Ramsden (10)
Holywell Green Primary School, Halifax

Friends
(Inspired by 'Ten Little Schoolboys' by A A Milne)

Ten friends waiting for the mall to open,
One saw a cute boy and then there were nine.
Nine friends in a shop looking at some clothes,
One saw a lovely top and then there were eight.
Eight friends having lunch in a posh restaurant,
One saw a puppy dog and then there were seven.
Seven friends having a drink of juice,
One saw her boyfriend and then there were six.
Six friends standing on some stairs,
One saw her mother and then there were five.
Five friends outside waiting for their ride,
One saw a taxi and then there were four.
Four friends in a minibus,
One went home and then there were three.
Three friends walking home,
One saw her father and then there were two.
Two friends jogging to the post office,
One saw her aunty and then there was one.
One friend running home,
One of her bags broke and then there was none.
No friends in the mall,
All together they sighed and that's the end of that.

Jacy Ellis (9)
Holywell Green Primary School, Halifax

Ocelot

Tree pouncer
Flesh ripper
Spotty camouflager
Prey gatherer
Tree hider
Soft kitten.

Katie Wilson (9)
Holywell Green Primary School, Halifax

Mums
(Inspired by 'Ten Little Schoolboys' by A A Milne)

Ten mums were standing in a line,
One saw some perfume and then there were nine.
Nine mums were walking behind the gate,
One saw a coffee stand and then there were eight.
Eight mums were getting on the bus to Heaven,
One saw a cheap offer and then there were seven.
Seven mums were looking at some chicks,
One saw some cows and then there were six.
Six mums were on TV live,
One saw a cute boy and then there were five.
Five mums were doing their chores,
One saw a pizza van and then there were four.
Four mums were growing a tree,
I saw a rose and then there were three.
Three mums were waiting for the loo,
One saw a scarf and then there were two.
Two mums were angry because of a con,
One saw a nest and then there was one.
One mum was on her way to see John,
She saw a Smart car and then there was none.

Rachel Smith (10)
Holywell Green Primary School, Halifax

My Sister

My sister is like a cuddly teddy bear,
She smells like lavender plants.
She is a good sister,
She's like a chick, here then there.
She is a little sister who's almost one year old,
She has a smelly nappy sometimes,
But the most important thing is that we love each other.

Jordan Bowers (10)
Holywell Green Primary School, Halifax

Ever Seen A (Rainforest)

Ever seen a jaguar high up in the sky?
Ever seen an anteater wearing a bow tie?
Ever seen a crocodile eating a pie?
Well, I have!
Ever seen a monkey washing in the shower?
Ever seen a sloth with a super power?
American flower.
Well, I have!
Ever seen a butterfly dancing on a ball?
Ever seen a tree frog wearing a pink shawl?
Ever seen a toucan in a shopping mall?
Well, I have!

Beth Ashton-Robson (10)
Holywell Green Primary School, Halifax

Cars

Subaru, Ford and Ferrari
Spark plugs lighting, tyres burning
Suspension bouncing, exhaust pumping
Steering wheel turning, brakes braking
Seats full of foam, gears at gear 6
Subaru, Ford and Ferrari

Cadillac Coupé de Villi
Car of the American dream
Cruising down Route 66
Crankshaft opening and shutting valves
Cadillac Coupé de Villi.

Joshua Gleadell (10)
Holywell Green Primary School, Halifax

The Jaguar

The jaguar is on the forest floor looking for prey
It goes in the river for a swim
The jaguar's prey is spotted, but it escapes
The jaguar camouflages again and patiently waits
It moves to a different location
It spots its prey again
The chase is on
It catches it . . .
Tears it
Yum!
Roar!

Daniel Smith (10)
Holywell Green Primary School, Halifax

Jaguar

Clever, speedy, spotty cat, races past the jungle trees.
Little, curious, frightened kitten, observant of what to do.
Fast, powerful creature, roams the dark, damp ground.
Smart, skilled runner pounces up high.
Skilful, intelligent jaguar, walks around carefully.
Loud, smooth, hairy little kitten.
Spotty, fast, cute animal.
Aware, powerful creature.
Little jaguar.
Alert!
Roar!

Jessica Smith (10)
Holywell Green Primary School, Halifax

My Best Friend

P aisley is very tall, Paisley is very loud, but most of all she's my best friend
A ll the time she makes me laugh, when I'm sad she makes me happy
I 'm always there for her, she's always there for me, but most of all she's my best friend
S ometimes we fall out, but we always get together again, she's the best
L onely I am, never, because Paisley is always there with me
E very time we play together and have sleepovers, but most of all she's my best friend
Y eah, she is my best friend.

April Willows (10)
Holywell Green Primary School, Halifax

Anteater

Digging, digging for an ant
Sniffing, sniffing all around
Licking, licking lips
Reaching above
Eating
Yum!

Jack Brudenell (11)
Holywell Green Primary School, Halifax

Leopard

Getting ready for his prey
It's found its prey
Sprints after a zebra
Fast runner
Pounces
Ow!

Haydn Corns (10)
Holywell Green Primary School, Halifax

Squirrel Monkey

It's a cute, cuddly fur ball
It's swinging to and fro
It's climbing up the branches to where it wants to go
Its fluffy tail falls behind
Its sticky hands cling on
It's hiding all around, nobody knows where it's gone
Now it's sleeping in a ball
Yes! It is a squirrel monkey, snug and small.

Michael Silvester (9)
Holywell Green Primary School, Halifax

Crocodile - Haikus

The croc is vicious
The sharp teeth feast on its prey
Their scaly, rough suit

It looks like a log
The claws stick into its prey
It is really big.

Jordan Thompson (9)
Holywell Green Primary School, Halifax

My Fabulous Life

My mansion is cosy and warm
With a roof and four walls
I own four acres of land
With five horses
I have a 50 inch telly
With a PS2 and a Wii
This is my fabulous life
I wish . . .

Ellie Rafton (9)
Longman's Hill CP School, Selby

My Playground

Silence
Whisper
Trees rustle in the breeze
Ding-dong!
Twelve o'clock
Children
Running
Like the wind
Shouting
Like a thunderstorm
Playing
Tig
Football
Catch
Toot! Toot!
A whistle
All gone
Silence
Whisper.

Lucy Crawford (10)
Longman's Hill CP School, Selby

Black Cat

Black cat,
Staring into the deep, dark sky.
Luminous eyes,
Glaring at us.
She's out to get,
Just me.
Those paws,
Like little feathers lightly hitting the ground.
Plod, plod.
Black fur,
Like the midnight sky.
Black cat.

Bethany Watson (11)
Longman's Hill CP School, Selby

Nothing To Think About

Blank
Nothing to think about
My mind's been stolen
There's a force . . .
Between my pen and paper
My brain won't work
Emotions rushing through my head
Worried,
Like losing a child
Fear,
Driving me
Tears,
Oozing down my face
Sweat,
Trickling down my back
Worried,
I can't write
Nothing to think about.

Erin Clark (11)
Longman's Hill CP School, Selby

What Am I?

What am I?
First things first.
I have a face but no head.
Second, I have hands but no arms.
I can be round or square,
Big or minute,
Loud or quiet and sometimes striking.
You can watch me but I will not go faster.
Your time and hours tick by.
What am I?

Jack Barker (10)
Longman's Hill CP School, Selby

The Clock

Tick-tock!
Tick-tock!
It's 4am.
The daylight is arriving, the birds are waking.
8am.
The cars are starting like a kettle on a morning.
It's 9 o'clock.
School and work are starting.
Tick-tock!
Tick-tock!
It's 12pm.
Dinner time. It's midday.
3pm.
Schools are finishing. The day gets louder.
It's 4 o'clock.
The streets are getting darker. Lamp posts start to glow.
8pm.
Kids settle down. Parents sit down to tea.
The world settles down.
Midnight.
The day has ended.

Oliver Bloxham (11)
Longman's Hill CP School, Selby

Sea

Waves are crashing
And the winds are howling
The sands are brushing by my face
Crabs are scuttling round my feet
Hurry! Hurry!
You hear them say
We must all scurry to hide away!
The sea!

Jake Douglas (10)
Longman's Hill CP School, Selby

Mysterious

A drift,
A splash,
Something walking
Through the sparkling water.
Won't hurt.
Raining fast,
Out of the water,
Riders daring,
Jumping,
Making it.
Cantering across
The bright,
Green grass,
Going down into a trot,
Rider gone,
Through the mist,
Never seen again!

Jessica Young (11)
Longman's Hill CP School, Selby

The Squirrel

The squirrel
Searching for nuts
He spirals up the oak tree
Storing nuts for winter
Snow starts to fall
The squirrel curls up
Into a ball of fluff
Spring comes
The squirrel is on the move.

Liam Foster (11)
Longman's Hill CP School, Selby

I Had An Argument

I had an argument with my friend today
It was over something silly
I said some things I shouldn't
I said sorry
She wouldn't listen.

I have no friends
I feel alone
She's getting all the attention
Teacher's walking closer
She calls my name
I always get the blame.

Teacher sat us down to talk
Sorry, sorry, I said over and over again
Tears started flowing
We made up.

I had an argument with my friend today
It was over something silly
I got upset, I felt alone
Teacher sat us down to talk
We made up.

Friends forever.

Georgia Southern (11)
Longman's Hill CP School, Selby

The Ocean

The water like diamonds
Lighting up the sea
White horses charging up to you
It flows like the wind
As if it's riding on dolphins.

Ben Moate (11)
Longman's Hill CP School, Selby

I'm Abandoned!

Alone
On the ground
Beneath the wall
Beside the door
Chained to the fence
    Purr!
Croaks a mew
Raises a paw
A bent oar
A tweaked whisker
Emerald eyes glare out from the darkness
Tiny tears on the ground
A cut paw
A slit tail
Lets out a little wail
Ouch, can't walk
Someone will find me somehow . . .

Kayleigh Richardson (10)
Longman's Hill CP School, Selby

Special Seasons

Summer's here, scream and shout
Let's tell them what it's all about.
Autumn, leaves fall from the trees
Catching a delightful, windy breeze.
Winter's here, it's Christmas at last
Just like the old days in the past.
Spring comes, animals say hello
In the wilderness below.

They all have fantastic reasons
This is why we have the seasons.

Rhianna MacDonald (10)
Longman's Hill CP School, Selby

Tests

The day has come
Tests galore, sweat coming
From every single part of my body
It's like I've just got out of a
Swimming pool
I could hear a mouse
Nibbling cheese
Tick
Tock
Tick
Tock
All I can hear
Is that stupid clock
Going fast
As sweat trickles down my back
Suddenly
The sweat stops oozing down my back
This is easy!

Harvey Rodgers (11)
Longman's Hill CP School, Selby

Sharks

A shark waiting for its prey
The prey not expecting anything
The shark getting ready
To force forward
3 . . .
2 . . .
1 . . .
The shark jumps out of the water
Catches the bird
Then drags it to the bottom
Of the ocean . . .
Yet again.

Sam Ness (10)
Longman's Hill CP School, Selby

Candyfloss

It's like a big ball of hair,
Usually found at the funfair.

You watch it getting made in a big metal cauldron,
As it is whirling it sounds really loud,
Till whips of candyfloss turn into a pink cloud.

Once you've got it, you don't know where to start,
You should always start at the best part.

When you bite into it,
It starts to melt.

Think of the fizziness you just felt.

You feel the magic,
But now it's all gone,
Which is rather tragic.

Just think of that taste,
The rest of it can't go to waste.

Olivia Scott (10)
Longman's Hill CP School, Selby

I Am Just A . . .

Hopping from tree to tree,
Do you know what I could be?

I hop around like a toad,
I don't say a single word.

I have fur and small ears,
Just remember, I don't have any fears.

I don't make a fuss,
I just gather nuts.

I am just a . . .

Scott Wilson (10)
Longman's Hill CP School, Selby

A Typical Morning

Snug in bed
Warm, cosy
Yawn
Stretch
Woken up
Need the loo!
Look in the mirror
Argh!
Bad hair day!
Go downstairs
Ow!
Argh!
Fell over
Eat breakfast
Swallowed vitamin
Yum, yum
Burp!
Get dressed
Scream!
Shout!
Had a fight
Kiss, kiss
Hug, hug
One for Mum
And one for Dad.

Anna Barrett (9)
Longman's Hill CP School, Selby

No School Today!

I'm not going to school today
I refuse!
I'm fed up every day
Following the rules.

I'm not going to school
I really don't want to
I know I'm acting like a fool
It makes me cry . . . *achoo!*

I'm not going to school
I really don't want to go
It's so uncool
To follow the rules.

I'm not going to school
No way
You really can't make me
Any day.

I'm not going to school
School's just a bore
I don't want any more.

I ended up going to school today
It was quite cool!

Courtney Chambers (9)
Longman's Hill CP School, Selby

The Big, Scary Creature

I'm thinking of a world inside my head
Although I'm lying in my bed.
I'm thinking of a big, scary creature
That has a rather special feature.
It's big and very scary
And very, very hairy.
It's as quiet as a mouse
When it's creeping into your house.
But when it comes in your room
It stomps with a boom!
I will tell you what this thing is later
But let me warn you, it's like an alligator!
If it hears us speak
We will be in hospital for a week.
You could even make that a year
Because it can taste your fear.
You can see it's as ugly as a blister
Because this thing is my . . . sister!

Mark Taylor (9)
Longman's Hill CP School, Selby

The Unhappy Soul

The beast was burning from inside the soul,
Now he's alone, he cannot reach his goal.
When he's performing, he looks so cold,
Even though he's not very old.

When the trainer comes with his whip,
I am surprised he doesn't make him trip.
When he jumps through the hoop,
People laugh when he doesn't finish the loop.

The trainer and his whip are so cruel,
When he's dreaming of meat you can see him drool.
He's being dragged down and down,
He's so unhappy and has the worst ever frown.

Ben Foster (11)
Northstead CP School, Scarborough

Life Of A Tiger

The creature is so sad,
But it's so seriously bad.
The disrespectful owner whipping him down and down,
While the audience are screaming and laughing, come all the way
                                                          from town.

The creature is approaching the crowd,
When they are shouting loud.
The horrible sight of the face,
Is not seen in the right place.

He's calm while he's standing straight,
Even while he looks at his bait.
A little girl comes up called Beth,
While his owner whips him to death.

Luke Sutcliffe (10)
Northstead CP School, Scarborough

Captivity

No one to love, no one to trust,
Keeping me in this tattered cage,
I must break free, I must, I must,
Keeping me in this world of rage.

Running free, running wild,
That's what I long for, that's what they took.
I want my son, my love, my child,
I want to hear my good friend's name.

They look, they point, they laugh, they shout,
My meal comes, I don't get much.
If I roar I get a clout,
I long for one gentle touch.

Jacob Hird (10)
Northstead CP School, Scarborough

The Performing Bear

Tortured, hurt, crouched on the cold, dusty floor,
Waiting for his trainer to open the cage door.
His muzzle strapped up like a child in a car,
Thinking of his homeland which is so far.

His belly rumbles so loud and clear,
As he walks on the stage with dreaded fear.
He performs his tricks like a silly old clown,
But finishes them with an endless frown.

He jumped and danced until he was battered and bruised,
Until the owner was completely amused.
The audience laughed and clapped with glee,
'If only they knew what it felt like to be me.'

Alaina Chambers (11)
Northstead CP School, Scarborough

The Tiger's Eye

The tortured soul lay there alone,
Its blood was boiling through its bone.
No longer even having a life,
What will happen to its children and wife?

Will they get taken away from their home?
Will they constantly groan and groan
Or will they just let them take them away?
I saw them just lay and lay.

The hunting car drove by fast,
I started thinking about the past.
The tiger's face was in a frown,
As he fell to the ground, down and down.

Catherine Hutchinson (10)
Northstead CP School, Scarborough

How Do Animals Feel?

Weary and alone, locked in a cage,
Fearing the trainer, knowing no friend.
For all twisted, full of rage,
The horrible feeling, coming to a bend.

Cries and screams approach like a hare,
From darkness to light, the end is near.
Trick after trick, no one to care,
Head hung low, with a twitching ear.

Performing like an amusing clown,
No love, no soul, no care.
The tearful animal being dragged down,
The killing pain, he cannot bear.

Zachary Slater (10)
Northstead CP School, Scarborough

Humiliated Animals

Ragged around like a dog's bone,
Silently he starts to moan.
They are so unkind,
The sad thing is some people don't mind.

This is not right, being treated like this,
It needs a kiss.
This is cruel,
But most of all, animals should rule!

He puts on a sad face,
Then he walks at a slow pace.
People pay to see these poor things,
He should be running round like a king.

Roxanne Cusworth (10)
Northstead CP School, Scarborough

The Heartbroken Creature

Bubbles erupting inside and out,
Head hung low, eyes look sore.
He feels pressure inside him which makes him want to shout,
Out in the crowd cruelty asks for more.

Body all gaunt, faded and foul,
The pitiable creature pondered why he was stuck in a portable prison.
Pouncing up onto the towering rails, he starts with rage to roar
                                              and growl,
As he's being lifted up, risen and risen.

Laughing and giggling out loud with glee,
Pathetic, uncared, beaten and whipped.
I am totally sure that won't happen to you and me,
As we are not animals, you see.
But as the neglected animal came down, it oh so gently slipped.

Ashleigh Pratt (10)
Northstead CP School, Scarborough

Entertainment Or Not?

His hurtful soul so full of fear,
So sad that the poor creature sheds a tear.
He's helpless and tired, so he pulls a frown,
And that's really getting me down.

His mouth is dry and muzzled,
If you look into his eyes, he looks puzzled.
The trainer is whipping away,
If I could, I would stop this any day.

The entertainment is poor,
I cannot watch this any more.
How can people watch this, aren't they ashamed?
The trainer is the only one to be blamed.

Sharna Cooper (10)
Northstead CP School, Scarborough

A Half Life

Lying down like the sand,
Sensing the beast approach him,
Bending down saying his demand,
While the tiger lies there grim.

As two strangers passed by,
They turned away and went through the door,
Four more people came through, one boy said, 'Hi,'
But the other laughed like a boar.

Suddenly, the beast came back,
I felt like I wanted to attack,
He gave me some meat,
Suddenly I was on my feet.
I ate the mouldy meat with one big gulp,
I scratched the bars and fell asleep.

Thomas McNally (11)
Northstead CP School, Scarborough

Tricky Tiger

The tortured soul no longer a goal,
Distraught, alone and upset.
The horrid trainer whipping holes,
But he's no longer a threat.

There he lay so big and bold,
The big, black cloud above his head.
He goes mad so people grab hold,
The beast never gets fed.

There he sits so bored and glum,
When he could be having loads of fun.
From friendly to fierce, no one knows,
It's like a great elephant hose.

Tyler Chapman (11)
Northstead CP School, Scarborough

The Last Minutes Of Your Life

Running through fields, like a horse on a racetrack,
Happy for a moment, but then he saw him,
The two-legged monster,
He freezes in fear, then runs.

Why did it have to be me? He says to himself.
Miserable and alone, he knows the end is near.

He's standing quiet as a mouse
And then the silence is gone.
Bang! The bullet hits him.
He lies on the ground, helpless and alone.
He takes his last breath and everything turns black.

William Gibson (10)
Northstead CP School, Scarborough

The Tortured Creature

The outraged look on the creature's face,
The steel jaws let him have no peace.
No swift end for the tortured beast,
The animal trapped like a great big feast.

The creature stood scratching with his claws,
The mouth of steel still nibbling at his paws.
The soul of the creature fading away,
The distraught creature dying day by day.

The horn he heard with his sharp, brown ears,
His cute little eyes making a river of tears.
The shaking of the ground he heard,
Getting shot like a wild bird.

James Deaves (10)
Northstead CP School, Scarborough

Dancing Bear

Dancing like a clown,
Dancing up and down,
Pain raging within, like the sun burning,
Pain within, like ice melting.

One foot in, one foot out,
Sadness in, sadness out.
Exciting for the people, not for the bear,
He wants to be free but does he dare?

The bear should be free,
But we stop them to have glee.
How would you like it if they made you dance?
How would you like it if they made you prance?

Jacob Stocks (10)
Northstead CP School, Scarborough

The Circus

Creeping, crawling in the tunnel
Sound growing like a funnel
Lift your leg, lift it high
The eagle soaring in the sky

The poor old beast, how does he cope?
Living his life without a hope
Travelling here, travelling there
Having to fight the grizzly bear

He's not that different from us
He is only a huge furry puss
It is unkind and now I don't feel well
Whoever does it should be locked in a cell.

Sophie Dent (10)
Northstead CP School, Scarborough

The Circus Tiger

Locked from home, fearing only the master,
As he approaches the tunnel, hoping to go faster.
From dark to light, the end is near,
He hears cries and screams from the side of the pier.

With no self will, he will have to do,
What only the mean master wants him to.
As he does his first trick, he wished to regret,
How quiet the crowd went, petrified as if they've just met.

The crowd being so selfish and sickening,
I sit there trembling with anger.
My blood vessels bubbling with hatred in my soul,
As he does his last trick, he triggers the owner's goal.

Thomas Brace (11)
Northstead CP School, Scarborough

Boxed In

Anger burning out of his soul,
Knowing he's never going to climb that hole.
Excitement is not part of his life,
He's never going to get a wife.

Trapped inside a cage only eight foot high,
With a sad face and a big sigh.
Always feeling sad and alone,
Never going back to his real home.

Now the sun is rising above,
People coming with a push and a shove.
Everyone moving here and there,
Most visitors looked at the grizzly bear.

Abigale Craig (11)
Northstead CP School, Scarborough

The Eyes Of The Creature

The eyes of the creature,
Watching, watching the crowd.
The whipping of the cane,
As the creature growls in pain.

The eyes of the creature,
Watching every soul.
Children screaming,
The eyes are beaming.

The eyes of the creature,
Watching every whip.
Listening to the babies' cries,
As the crowd say their goodbyes.

Hayley Towell (10)
Northstead CP School, Scarborough

The Sobbing Bear

He staggered onto the roaring stage,
Trapped in a tiny, suffocating cage.
With a face like thunder he began the show,
Wearing a coat that looked like snow.

The crowd jumped and shouted with glee,
As the poor, beaten animal wished to be free.
The cracked heart started to break even more,
His legs were bruised, battered and sore.

Feeling neglected and all alone,
He sat and had a moan and a groan.
As the trainer stood tall and proud,
He beat the beast to please the crowd.

Lucy Hirstle (11)
Northstead CP School, Scarborough

Boo!

We go to Ravensworth school,
The teachers are really cool.
We jump up and down,
But never frown
Unless we are really down.

The teachers are really rockin',
They never made us do blockin'.
They're here all day
And do nothing but play
And do whatever we say.

We go to the office by leaping
And find the teachers all sleeping.
The excuses they make and do
Are obvious by just one clue.
All we have to do is just shout . . .
Boo!

Toni Hutchinson & Ellie Blenkiron (11)
Ravensworth CE Primary School, Richmond

Friendship

I'll always be beside you,
Until the very end,
Wiping all your tears away,
Being your best friend.
I'll smile when you smile,
Feel all the pain you do,
And if you cry a single tear,
I promise I'll cry too.

If you find Molly, you'll find Ruth,
They never lie to each other,
They always tell the truth,
We'll be friends forever,
Do you think we'll split up? *Never!*

Ruth Bernard & Molly Maddison (9)
Ravensworth CE Primary School, Richmond

If The World Were Made Of Chocolate

If the world were made of chocolate,
We would have no door,
If the world were made of chocolate,
There would be no floor.

If the world were made of chocolate,
We wouldn't have a roof,
If the world were made of chocolate,
Trust me, you would have a sweet tooth.

If the world were made of chocolate,
You would be fat and plump,
If the world were made of chocolate,
You wouldn't have a grump.

Chloe Barrett (11)
Ravensworth CE Primary School, Richmond

If I Could Fly

If I could fly,
I'd cross the world
And be back home for tea.

If I could fly,
I'd fly up to Venus, Mars and Pluto
And maybe even the sun.

If I could fly,
I'd fly with all the birds
And all the flying insects.

If I could fly,
I'd fly in winter, summer, autumn and spring
And enjoy the different weather.

Abby Metcalfe (10)
Ravensworth CE Primary School, Richmond

Dinosaurs

D inosaurs have camouflage and they have sharp, scary teeth
I like dinosaurs because they have fights and they have brains
   the size of a peanut
N obody wants to stand in front of a dinosaur because it will *eat you!*
O nly a million years ago could you see dinosaurs
S ome dinosaurs were herbivores and others were carnivores
A lways remember that they are vicious
U nless you find a dinosaur you will never know how vicious they are
R emember, *stay away!*

Alexander James Lillie (9)
Ravensworth CE Primary School, Richmond

Army

A rmy are very brave because they might get killed
R ecruits and medics, all the lot, but one thing, they might get shot
M ines and bazookas, both make a big *bang!*
Y ucky trenches with dead people in, you hope that you're not
   the next one in!

Ben Tennant & Will Turnbull (10)
Ravensworth CE Primary School, Richmond

Special Star

Special star
Special star
Shining high in the sky
Shining light, singing night
Can I ride my horse tonight?

Victoria Marcelino-Purse (10)
Ravensworth CE Primary School, Richmond

Family

F amily is there for you
A nd I have a mum, dad and a sister too
M y sister is sometimes loud and funny
 I have a grandma and grandad who like to give me money
L ots of family is not too much for
Y ou!

Bethaney Rush (10)
Ravensworth CE Primary School, Richmond

Bubblebee

Bubblebee collecting money
Bubblebee eating honey
Bubblebee whizzing so fast
Bubblebee having a task
Bubblebee go away
Come back another day.

Lauren Kemp (10)
Ravensworth CE Primary School, Richmond

Swimming

Swimming is my sport,
Swimming is my thing,
Swimming is my fantasy,
Hey ding-a-ling-a-ling.

At home I get lots of support,
My coach is really cool,
Training here, training there,
Throughout every year.

Rachel Stirr (11)
Ravensworth CE Primary School, Richmond

What Am I?

I live in the zoo
I swing in the trees
I am sometimes cheeky
And you can't tell me what to do.
I eat bananas
I love them a lot
I can do lots of tricks
Can you guess what I am?

Chloé Burrows (10)
Ravensworth CE Primary School, Richmond

Dogs

D is for dogs running around all day
O is for jumping over walls
G is for going crazy
S is for super good at rounding up sheep.

Adam Wallis (10)
Ravensworth CE Primary School, Richmond

Striker

Handstanding goal shooter scores a goal in a hole
Good striker. It is a good match, Manchester United win
The smoke blowin', players slidin' everywhere
Have a crash and the super goalie
Saves the ball
And it is a rainy day
The crowd are sad
Because their
Team
Has
Lost.

Mackenzie Charlesworth (8)
St Joseph's RC Primary School, Doncaster

Fear

I send a spider to make your hair stand on end.
I make you cover your face during a scary film.
I cause panic when you see a wasp.
I send a shiver down your body.
I make you have goosebumps when you see my shadow.
I creep up behind you when you aren't looking.
I make your teeth chatter when you're scared.
I send a nightmare to scare you at night.
I am fear!

Daniel McDonnell (10)
St Joseph's Primary School, Pontefract

Fear

I am the one who sends you phobias
I turn you cold when you hear bad news
I make your nightmares unforgettable
I trick your mind and give you horrors
I destroy your laughs and change them to screams
I send the spiders to crawl up your arm
I send the darkness to spook you at night
I place a creepy shadow behind you
    I am fear!

Callum Hughes (10)
St Joseph's Primary School, Pontefract

Football

I love the atmosphere at Elland Road
I enjoy being a fan
I like the strikers scoring goals
Beckford is the top scorer
At the games I eat burgers and chips
I own a season ticket
My wish is to go to Wembley and see them win the cup.

Ben Booth (10)
St Joseph's Primary School, Pontefract

Happiness

I give you a magical feeling on a cheerful Christmas Day.
I send a chuckle to a smiling baby's face.
I make a brightly coloured flower bloom on a summer's day.
I make a worm wriggle, I take your dream and turn it into a reality.
I give a mother a baby to care for.
I give you a feeling that you never want to go away.
    I am happiness.

Helen Walsh (10)
St Joseph's Primary School, Pontefract

Fear

I send a shiver down your spine.
I make you screech louder than thunder.
My screams make your hair stand on end.
I send a creepy shadow that follows you at night.
I make you freeze when you are scared.
I send a nightmare of your worst terrors.
I send you horrors that haunt you forever.
I addict you to nicotine so you can't stop.
I am fear!

Joseph Paul Taylor (10)
St Joseph's Primary School, Pontefract

Sadness

I am the tear which trickles down your face.
I play the song which makes you sob.
I scrape your knee upon the floor.
I demolish the beautiful glass which you cherished.
I shatter your friend's heart with my actions.
I shriek the words that hurt your feelings.
I raise your hopes and smash them dearly.
I snatch the person you love without thought.
    I am sadness.

Natalya Wilson (10)
St Joseph's Primary School, Pontefract

Space

The sun's hair curves and spikes
As comets brush by.

As the planets spy on each other,
They wonder where the monster is.

As the black hole
Gobbles anything in its path.

It remains silent
Except for a few slurps of comets
That have passed by.
It lives in darkness,
Waiting for food.

Saturn's ring wraps around its neck
Like a scarf.
It is lonely,
It is waiting for a friend.

As it prowls and lurks
On the other planets,
Until it eats them.

The planet monster is running.
Hide before he gets you.

Tyler Wright (10)
Sandringham Primary School, Doncaster

At The Beach

The shore brushes the seaweed roughly,
Massive caves listen to the echoing of the boats,
A lighthouse blinks as a warning,
Calm seas wave in the air.
Soft sand wears the millions of shells as jewellery,
Lots of boats scream as they head near the rocks,
Miniature caves slurp up the water as quickly as they can.

Shannon Smith (11)
Sandringham Primary School, Doncaster

The Ocean

The deep ocean thinks in his coral brain,
Spiky iceberg hair floats in the morning sun,
His rock pool eyes peer over the coming tide,
Spying sailed intruders,
He chomps on a giant sandwich with his huge mouth.

His mighty hands climb up chalky cliffs,
As he slurps the coming rain.
Island ears listen in on the wind's eerie song,
The warm Pacific wears a misty silhouette
In the morning light.

Thousands of compact ants crawl up his wavy back,
In the summer, accompanied by trawlers,
Come to feast on his luxurious bounty.
As the sun sets behind his indigo back,
He says goodnight.

Edward Miles (11)
Sandringham Primary School, Doncaster

Le Mountain

The mountain's peak towers high above the clouds.
Rocks tumbling down, fall like an elevator shooting downwards.
Its steep edges provide platforms for the occasional rest.
Hundreds of shabby, grey rocks
With iron rods scattered for people to walk on.
The Eiffel Tower's pointy tip undergoes blizzards during winter.
Smooth sides are outrun by rocks and razor-sharp wires.
Mountains take caution to be sure of no rust.
The Eiffel Tower crumbles after hundreds of years
Standing high above the city of Paris.
Mountains still above the clouds, last longer than the tower.

Helen Wilson (10)
Sandringham Primary School, Doncaster

Volcano

The volcano stands alone like a solitary chimney,
Smoke rising from a single funnel.

The sky is darkened with smoke,
Clouds dotted with red specks.

Furnaces roaring with bubbling lava,
The gaping mouth starts to spit.

A sudden gush and a rush for the door,
The lava spills over the open space.

Hours and hours, burning itself out,
The volcano comes to a halt!

The years have taken their toll,
Now the mighty volcano is finally derelict,
Ash-covered plains are the only reminder
Of its enormous power.

Connor Martin (10)
Sandringham Primary School, Doncaster

The Volcano

The lava is spilling over the sides of the erupting volcano,
It's boiling all the time.
Plane wheels bouncing up and down quickly,
As they float in the lava spreading down the volcano.
The conveyor belt is moving all the time,
Transporting crusty rocks down the rigid side.
Steps left by black, burning rock,
As it cools all over the crumbling volcano.
When the lava reaches the bottom of the volcano,
All of the black, burning rock rushes to the floor.

Charlotte Nesbitt (11)
Sandringham Primary School, Doncaster

The Old Willow Tree

In the middle of the crowded forest,
In a clearing far away,
There stands a lonely willow tree.

Leaves drape over her enormous face,
Bugs cover her like a raincoat,
And even though she is surrounded by trees,
She is lonely.

The birds' nests that are perched in her branches,
Remind her of old and happy memories.

Her silent mouth is residence to tawny owls,
Her feet are all knotted, as they dig down into the solid earth.
Long arms drag along the barren ground.

Blustery weather causes her elderly leaves to whistle piercingly
Through the chilly air,
Drizzle slowly covers her face,
Converting it from contentment to tearfulness.

Paige Williams (11)
Sandringham Primary School, Doncaster

The Turtle

The miniature pod shuffles along the barren ground,
Like an oval shell coming to a halt.
With a little help from its dawdling arms,
Which suddenly swing back into action
And start to move leisurely.
Gradually, after time,
It returns to its home and plods away
Through the grassy fields, solemnly,
Making humming sounds and trundling round and round.

Georgia Morton (11)
Sandringham Primary School, Doncaster

Helicopter

The propellers wave rapidly in the sky
As the helicopters hover above the tall skyscrapers.

When the helicopter starts up,
He begins to noisily hum.

His windows stare up and down bleakly
At the objects below and above him.

His door opens wide
To let people in to be devoured.

On return, after his prolonged flight,
He likes to have his coat of paint changed.

He's very shy about most people seeing him close,
So he hides away up in the clouds.

Jumping up and down, excited about his journey,
With engines roaring, he shoots off again.

Liam Davies (11)
Sandringham Primary School, Doncaster

Beach

The boats scream as they head for the rocks.
A cave listens to the echoing of the boats humming.
Gigantic lighthouse blinks at the boats to warn them.

Wild oceans brush the seaweed, as the tide comes in.
Tonnes of sand wears the millions of shells left behind.

Deep blue sea, in the air as a cave slurps it up.

Jake Lockwood (11)
Sandringham Primary School, Doncaster

The Castle

The castle has a scary skeleton face
Terrifying the intruders
Around the castle

The scared knights
Show their glowing shield
Which reflects the moon

The stars reflect their twinkling body
On the shining armour

The moon hovers above the ground
While bloodthirsty dogs
Scramble to get the knight

There are terrifying gargoyles
Below the castle wall

Behind the moon
It looks like a dark, gloomy dungeon

The moon is as high as a castle tower
It has a colourful flying flag.

Ryan Ellis (10)
Sandringham Primary School, Doncaster

Mountain

Mountain doors, carved with arched sandstones.
Ancient rocks have been crumbled by the narrow paths.
A pyramid's point, surrounded by gritty sand.
Overhead is the bright sky,
Shimmering towards the rough bricks.
Steps loop around,
Puzzling mankind as they travel up its steep, rocky wall.

Bethany Atkinson (11)
Sandringham Primary School, Doncaster

Space

Comets shooting in the sky,
Above the Earth oh, so high.

Gasses hissing on Venus,
It's quite noisy - don't forget your ear muffs.

Sun gazing down at Earth,
It's looking for water to evaporate.

Jupiter spinning like a Ferris wheel,
At the fairground.

Planets whisper to each other,
I think they might be playing Chinese whispers.

Dust balls revolving, revving up,
Getting ready to attack the stars.

Lucy Davison (10)
Sandringham Primary School, Doncaster

The Mansion

The mansion glimmers like shiny bricks.
It has brightly polished doors.
It has a grand spiral staircase,
With spotless marble floors.

The mansion has a king-size four-poster bed.
It has a fresh flowing waterfall
In the landscaped garden,
With a square-shaped swimming pool.

The mansion has beautifully decorated windows.
It has smooth, curved chairs,
With candles in the middle of the humungous table.

Diben Pun (11)
Sandringham Primary School, Doncaster

The Library

The library has dusty books,
Sitting on the old bookshelves.
Its books fill the restricted area.

Its dull lights shine down
On the horror books,
High up on the shelves.

Its two lonely receptionists,
Work at the desks all day long.

Its sliding ladders move around,
As the old, crooked man
Sorts out the books.

Its carpets bulge, full with dust,
As the cleaner clears it up.

Rebecca Thirlwell (11)
Sandringham Primary School, Doncaster

The Dreaded Ball Wall

Deep down in the playground,
Where the ball wall lay,
Children play football,
From morning to day.

The clouds are his afro,
He wears three coats of paint,
When the teachers see him,
They almost nearly faint.

He hesitates for the children,
Waiting to jump,
The children don't come out,
So he starts to slump.

Adam Kean (11)
Sandringham Primary School, Doncaster

The Mansion

The mansion has old, creaking doors.
Its murky, arched windows are aged with time.

Its dirty, damaged attics,
Hold dead, rotting bodies
And dusty old skeletons.

The chipped pottery sits on the historic mantelpiece,
As they attract the dust.

Its floor holds tatty rugs,
As they weep with time.

The walls are coated
With devilish-looking gargoyles.

Its corridors blanketed with rusty, worn out armour,
As they stare at passing trespassers.

And finally, its shattered chandeliers
Cover the floor.

Aisha Miller (11)
Sandringham Primary School, Doncaster

The Solar System

The mysterious tombstones cover the open black space.
Hmmm?

Asteroids flee across the misty space,
Jumping from page to page.
Hmmm?

A cluster of stars attending the funeral, is a nebula.

Bradley Maltby (10)
Sandringham Primary School, Doncaster

The Library

The library has a bouncy bell,
That tings all day long.

Its organised cupboards,
Clash as the librarian walks in.

Its pesky flies and other insects,
Annoy the visitors.

The library's health and safety advertisements,
Talk to the children.

Its good quality books,
Shimmer in the light.

Its mouldy roof,
Spoils the great look.

The library's air fans,
Blow you away.

Its bold bricks,
Smarten up the building.

Its spinning computer chairs,
Relax and soothe you.

Jordan Quinn (10)
Sandringham Primary School, Doncaster

Mountain

The stony, rocky mountain,
Towering towards the shiny sun.
The lanky, rough, rocky mountain,
Echoes to the space outside.
The abandoned creatures feel cold,
Inside the frosty, snowy mountain.

Dominik Tylicki (10)
Sandringham Primary School, Doncaster

The Old, Scruffy Sports Car

The old scruffy sports car,
Inhabits a lonely garage.

It wears orange spray paint,
With red bumper stickers.

Its black, bendy interior,
Goes side to side in the wind.

As it goes along the road,
It eats all the tarmac.

Its scruffy, rubber wheels,
Go as fast as lightning.

Its red, dim lights,
Are very beady.

Its mouth is its bonnet,
It goes up and down like it's eating something.

When its horn goes - it's shouting,
It's got a really deep voice.

Liam Simmons (10)
Sandringham Primary School, Doncaster

The Castle

The castle has a steep staircase.
Its rusty, steel chains dangle from the rooms.
Its rooms have old, rotten, dead bodies on the floor.

Its bloodthirsty lions eat the dead people.
Its rigid battlements look out for enemies.

It has scary skeletons on the floor.
Its unbreakable dungeon keeps the smell of blood.
Its squeaky wooden doors open by themselves.

Matthew Jewell (10)
Sandringham Primary School, Doncaster

The School

The school has grumpy teachers,
Moody, strict head teacher sits in her office.

Its small corridors wind along,
Past terrifying toilets haunted by tales.

The enormous classrooms engulf the small children,
Its neat tables lined up like soldiers,
Its overflowing pen pots sit in clutter.

Its bookshelves tidy and neat,
Full of knowledge and information.

Its bell echoes down the corridor,
Its doors stream with children.

The school is silent and empty again.

Rebecca Wynne (10)
Sandringham Primary School, Doncaster

Space

Jupiter spins like a Ferris wheel, making her feel dizzy.
The gas hisses, as it snakes around on Venus,
Eliminating everything in its path.
Dust rotating from one planet to another,
A monstrous bowling ball, gathering speed,
Ready for a strike.
The comets shoot across the sky,
Playing football with the stars.
Earth is frying in a pan
As the sun is glaring down.
Planets whisper to each other,
Playing games to combat boredom.

Caitlin Bower (10)
Sandringham Primary School, Doncaster

The Mansion

The mansion has huge, towering doors,
With the windows that are cracked.

Its trees are long, dark and windy.
Its dungeons are filled with skeleton bones.

Ghosts hover up and down,
All around the dead plants and tombstones.

The mansion's chef is grubby,
As he cooks dinner!

It sneezes, *atishoo,* at the dusty shelves,
Mingled with the books.

The mansion is a murky old river,
As dead fish float on the top!

Its maids scamper around,
Cleaning the messy bedrooms.

Bethany Alton (11)
Sandringham Primary School, Doncaster

Beatrude, The Pink Car

As the horn speaks,
And the doors creak,
Beatrude talks to another car
And they agree to ride on some dancing tar.

They stopped for some petrol
And Beatrude adjusted her aerial
As they danced the night away.

The other car,
Took Beatrude back on the tar
And the other car watched her,
While she slept in a deep, deep sleep.

Shelby Amess (10)
Sandringham Primary School, Doncaster

The Pub

The people in the pub are picking
At the pork scratchings.

It has children jumping
Enthusiastically in the play area.

It has OAPs lazing about
In the lounge area.

Its barmaids pulling forcefully
At the stiff beer pumps.

It has people changing the beer barrels
Down in the cellar.

It has centurions having a pint
And a packet of prawn cocktail crisps.

It's got teenagers drinking a Coke
And having a little gossip outside.

Jack Burton (10)
Sandringham Primary School, Doncaster

The Airport

The airport has humungous planes,
Bustling passport controllers,
Who are really strict.

The runway is as bumpy as the speed bumps
On the road.

The pubs are active with drunken passengers.
People are overcrowded in the duty free shops.

Passengers are getting delayed,
So they are passing the time in posh restaurants.

The car parks are busy with cars,
There is no more room.

The busy shuttle bus is ferrying passengers
To the correct terminal.

Jordan Jackson (10)
Sandringham Primary School, Doncaster

The Castle

The castle holds scary skeletons
Terrifying the intruders

Its narrow, firing loops
Spit out at you

Its rusty chains rot
As more people come in
Time after time

Its knights and shiny armour
Glisten in the sunlight

Its dark dungeons smell
Of rotting, dead bodies

Its bloodthirsty lions
Lick their lips
As people get thrown in one by one

Its terrifying gargoyles
Stare at you wherever you go.

Kelly Baxendale (10)
Sandringham Primary School, Doncaster

The Unbeatable Car

Its headlights are like
Little beady eyes

It lives in a lonely garage
Next to an abandoned farmhouse

Its hair is all folded up
Like a black, crinkled blanket

It comes out at night
'Cause it doesn't like the light

It wears a shiny new metal coat
Like when dew settles on a rose petal.

Matthew Jones (11)
Sandringham Primary School, Doncaster

The Airport

The airport has humungous, deafening planes.
Its bumpy runways drag the bags over to the plane.

Its passport control is really strict,
With clattering tickets.

The pubs are bustling
With drunken passengers.

It's packed with duty free shops,
People shouting and thumping.

Its passengers are delayed in the restaurants,
Waiting for the planes.

The car parks are overcrowded with people watching children.
Its viewing lounge is filled with children,
Glaring through the window.

Its busy shuttle buses,
Ferrying passengers to the terminals.

The conveyor belts overloaded with heavy suitcases.
People banging up and down the steps,
As they step out of the plane.

Ears popping when they go around in circles,
As they eat their prawn cocktail crisps.

Phoebe Grantham (10)
Sandringham Primary School, Doncaster

Fairy

The fairy is as light as a lark's feather.
She sparkles like raindrops in the sun.
Her wings flutter like butterflies in the breeze.
The fairy is as small as a mouse's paw
And as beautiful as a rosebud.

Beth MacDonald (8)
South Cave CE Primary School, Brough

Beautiful Rainbow

Beautiful bright colours floating in the sky,
With clouds at each end.
It only comes out when it's rainy and sunny,
Will it come out again?
I hear it singing in a high-pitched voice,
Floating in the sky.

It feels so soft, cosy and cuddly,
It feels like you're in bed with your teddy bear.
You could never guess how soft it is,
You could live on it because it's so soft.
But you need to be careful because you might fall through,
It's not that thick!

The colours are so bright, like a colourful butterfly
Floating in the sky.
You can see it from far, far away.
It is surrounded by clouds.
Can you guess what it is yet?

Lucy Lowther (9)
South Cave CE Primary School, Brough

Teddy Bear

Teddy you make my heart,
Teddy you're like a star that guides me,
If my house was on fire it would break my heart to leave you,
Teddy, teddy you're my own forever,
I love my teddy and I think he loves me too,
Brown and fluffy, your eyes twinkle,
You're soft and your scarf is green and red.

Dean Makowski-Clayton (8)
South Cave CE Primary School, Brough

The Creeping Crocodile

His eyes so beady, big and bold,
His scales so slimy, shiny and cold,
His teeth so sharp and scary,
Like big swords,
His tail so snappy and strong,
It looks unbreakable,
Like a metal pole.

Gliding through the lake,
He camouflages in,
His green and brown coat,
Like weeds floating around,
He creeps around the forest,
When you never know.

His home so green,
With bones all around,
He sleeps and snores,
So loud like a jingling tambourine,
You should always watch out,
When the creeping crocodile's about.

Lucy Reast (9)
South Cave CE Primary School, Brough

Stone

Strange stone,
You are as hard as the Earth's crust
Still like a guardian.

How do you get around?
You are everywhere,
Beach, walls, mountains,
You are everywhere.

To an ant you are like a mountain
You come in all sizes.

Harvey Plows (8)
South Cave CE Primary School, Brough

Noisy Dogs

Oh dogs, why do you never stop barking?
It is always *bark, bark, bark.*
All you have to do is be quiet.
Some dogs are the best, they're quiet,
They hate biting but you, you adore barking and biting.

Dogs as noisy as a lion,
Puppies as cute as a monkey,
Cute dogs just like a cuddly tiger,
Dogs coming towards you like a cheetah.

What is your favourite type of dog?
Is it a cute little Labrador or a ferocious golden retriever?
Lots of dogs are cute, just choose the right one please!

Ruth Dobson (8)
South Cave CE Primary School, Brough

Mythical Creatures

Have you seen a two-headed lion who can blow fire
When he roars like a plane flying by, heading to war?
They are scary like fighter jets firing massive missiles
Fast as a bullet, ready to blow up their victim.

Have you ever seen a squirrel, with a thousand eyes?
They are very small, but very strong like lions.
Flying lions, deathly, deadly and dangerous,
Speaking their languages, roaring like a bell.
Could you fight? Would you win?
No one knows, for who has seen a two-headed lion?

Finlay Hills (8)
South Cave CE Primary School, Brough

Homework

Before I do my homework
I think I'll watch TV
Before I do my homework
I'll watch the film ET.

Before I do my homework
I'll play on my PS3
Before I do my homework
I'll go on my Nintendo Wii.

Before I do my homework
I'll run right up the stairs
Before I do my homework
I'll make some chocolate pears.

Uh-oh, it's nearly bedtime
Oh no, it's time for tea
If I don't get it finished
My teacher will shout at me!

Madeleine Borman (8)
South Cave CE Primary School, Brough

Bedtime Monster

When it is time for bed,
The monster comes out from beside my bed
He is as black as night
And has silver spikes
To scare the little boys and girls away.

Every night I always have to go through this,
Slam the doors
To try and make him go away
But it's not working!

Hannah Ozsanlav (8)
South Cave CE Primary School, Brough

Bedtime Nightmares

Every night I go to bed thinking of bad dreams,
I think about grizzly ghosts coming every night,
I dream about everything really,
But I never want to stop dreaming,
It's just too hard to stop!

When I'm sleeping deeply,
I can never wake up,
Unless I get scared,
I always turn on the light,
When I wake up I feel someone watching me,
Right from behind!

I feel something weird on my back,
Listen, you might hear it,
It might be something black,
It could be a ghost,
Argh! Watch out!

Aimee Olsson (9)
South Cave CE Primary School, Brough

Dolphins

Whenever I see a dolphin
They wet me with a splash!
Whenever I see a dolphin
My dad has gone in a flash.

Whenever I see a dolphin jump
They make me feel like a kangaroo.

Whenever I see a dolphin dive
They make me feel like I'm diving in the pool.
Whenever I see a dolphin splash
They make me feel nice and cool.

Hollie Ferguson-Pratt (8)
South Cave CE Primary School, Brough

Colours

Colours are beautiful,
Colours are bright.
I know a colour,
It is blank and it's called white.

Colours are beautiful,
Colours are so light.
And some are bold,
As yellow gold.

Colours are remarkable,
As lovely as can be.
Colours are so radiant,
There is a colour called grassy green.

Colours are so elegant,
As fine as can be.
Colours are attractive,
They're all I need to see.

William Joseph Branagan (8)
South Cave CE Primary School, Brough

Chocolate

The colours are very creamy
Smooth and so watery
Brown and absolutely squidgy.

When I finish I want another
But if I have ten chocolate bars
Very fat and sick will I be!

Chocolate, chocolate,
Don't have another
Because you will be . . .
Poorly!

George Thornham (8)
South Cave CE Primary School, Brough

Ghosts And Monsters

Each night when I go to bed,
And cuddle up tightly to my ted,
I feel that I need to make noises,
To scare away the monster.
But he never goes away,
I really, really, wish he would today.

As I lie asleep, my dreams ponder
Dreaming of only ghosts and a monster.
Dreaming really deeply, I cannot wake up.
I awake to the peer of that monster
That lies beneath my bed.
A monster with purple spikes upon his head
Bright orange eyes and as black as the night.
He only comes when it's dark to scare the boys and girls.

I feel something as I turn under my covers.
Something or someone under my bed.
I fear and quickly pull the covers over my head.

Shannon O'Loughlin (8)
South Cave CE Primary School, Brough

My Dog Ate My Homework

My dog ate my homework yesterday.
My heart sunk with sadness,
I was like a volcano erupting.
I thought, *oh no, I will have to go to school with no homework.*
I went to school, the teacher bellowed.
'Where is your homework?'
'I'm sorry Miss, my dog ate my *homework!*'

Tom Watson (9)
South Cave CE Primary School, Brough

The Kitten Taker

A stranger knocked on the door
He was like a bat
I was scared
His shoes were undone
He came in and stole my kitten
I started to cry.

Now when I see people dressed in black
It makes me want to cry.

I found her lying on the ground
I thought she was dead
I was crying like mad
But then I heard her miaow
I was so happy until that man came and kicked her
She was crying
I was crying
Last time I saw her there was only a tail!

Elizabeth Haigh
South Cave CE Primary School, Brough

The Bedtime Monster

Did you hear the monster?
His feet crashing down as he stepped up the stairs
A large crack
I thought that was what he was going to do to my back
Thud, thud!
I could hear him approach the door
His fur was like a big ball of cotton
But when he gets you
It's all over . . .

Jack Henderson (9)
South Cave CE Primary School, Brough

Running

When I'm at the start
I'm shaking like a leaf
But when I get the rhythm
I'm running as fast as a cheetah.

I never want to stop
So when I come to the end
I feel up high
But down low

I could run forever; day and night
There's only one problem
I would collapse, my heart bumping
Like a red juicy apple, falling off a tree.

It's the end
Of my running
I'll be racing again soon
I'm sure!

Eleanor Raitt (9)
South Cave CE Primary School, Brough

Scared Of The Football

When I play football, my sisters run
They go inside and tell my mum
I try to hide in a bush
But they always shove and push
They always find me
And tell me off!

When I play football my sisters tell my dad
I try to get out of trouble
But there's no way out
When he tells me off
I feel like . . .

Louis Stevenson (8)
South Cave CE Primary School, Brough

The White Bunny

On the ice I felt sunny
Swirling and twirling all around.
But when I saw a big white bunny
I fell over on the ground.

I picked myself up
And fell back down.
Then the big white bunny
Hopped into town.

I chased him
All around the square.
Then the bunny
Hopped with the hare.

Then at last
I caught the bunny.
But he thought
It was oh so funny.

So when I got home
The bunny was on the phone
But when the bunny kissed my mummy
That was the funniest of all.

That night I sat in my room wondering
Why was the bunny on the ice?
I thought that chasing the bunny
Was like chasing my sister.
Was it . . . ?
Couldn't be.

Georgia Eve Smith (8)
South Cave CE Primary School, Brough

Rocking Robots

Rocking rolling Ryan rattles to and fro,
Rolling rocking Ryan roars to go slow,
If you see rocking rolling Ryan rattling,
Try and take care!

His eyes are orange like burning fire,
They light up in the night,
So don't be afraid because,
If you are, you're not brave!

If he is enchanted, he might be quite kind,
He might be made of magic,
Who knows, he's probably like
Some kind of gadget!

He's orange, red, green and gold,
He's like a roaring lion,
So don't be terrified, just be brave,
And you'll survive!

Emma Williamson (8)
South Cave CE Primary School, Brough

Football Crazy

When I play football I feel I lose all the time.
People are scared of the ball and foul all the time.
I fall over the ball all the time.
I fall over my shoelaces, they're never tied.
I never keep clean, I hate my baths!
One day my team will win.
I-I-I-I can't take it anymore!
I want to win some day like . . . tomorrow!

Kristian White (8)
South Cave CE Primary School, Brough

Colours Of A Stone

An emerald as green as grass
A ruby as red as blood
A sapphire as blue as Heaven
A flint lies in the mud

Emerald, ruby, sapphire and flint
All make colours, even pink

A diamond is a brilliant stone
To catch the world's desire
But flint holds a fire deep inside
Waiting to be ignited.

Joshua Moore (8)
South Cave CE Primary School, Brough

In The Garden

In the garden where I play,
The sky is blue and the path is grey,
I ride my bike round the rockery,
I look in the mud and see some pottery.

In the garden we grow apples on the trees,
And they blow in the breeze.
I play football against my dog
I trip over the ball and see a hedgehog!

Jade Smith (9)
South Cave CE Primary School, Brough

Cats

Every day I see my cat
In and out, finding friends,
In the night he comes in
Licking my face to bits,
In the morning he's still there.

Every day I see my cat,
Licking his mouth, then he goes outside
Looking for his girlfriend
My cat is white, brown and black
But I feel so bad
Because he has a bad eye.

Chloe Hiles (9)
South Cave CE Primary School, Brough

Morning Job

I wake up.
The sky is grey and rainy.
It's a bad day.
I have my breakfast.
Wash my face
And brush my teeth.
I am now ready for the day.
My job is awful
Because I have to fix everything.
I'm sure you wouldn't like it.
I work in a theme park.

Tobias Pometsey (8)
South Cave CE Primary School, Brough

Ferocious Floods

There's black murky water,
Roaring down the street,
Thunder's growling,
Mayhem is building.
Grannies are floating down the street.

The water flows like a snake,
But everything in its path is destroyed.
Oh when will the water end
Gushing down the street?

Ben Sage (8)
South Cave CE Primary School, Brough

The Windy Wet Weather

The rain pattered so hard,
It sounded as loud as a cymbal,
And the grumbling loud wind crashed,
It was so loud, it could tear your hair.

Yet all of this but the glittering snow,
Was as quiet as a feather,
Never go out in the pouring rain
Or your hair will look bad.

Fay Inverarity (8)
South Cave CE Primary School, Brough

Have You Ever Seen A Genie?

Have you ever seen a kind blue genie?
Has he ever granted you three wishes?
Is his lamp nice and golden brown?
Can he give you a joyful laugh?
Have you ever seen a kind blue genie?

Oliver Drake (9)
South Cave CE Primary School, Brough

Space

Space is like a fat hippo
Space is like a bumpy camel
Space is a big, black, dark world
When you speak in space
You always get an echo
In space it's cold and dark
Dark like the night sky with no moon
Space is white and freaky black
Stars tinkle in the dark sky
Planets bouncing through the dark night
Would you like to live in space?

Sam Moment (8)
South Cave CE Primary School, Brough

The Football Pitch

In the football ground, they sing like girls.
The match starts and they all scream and shout.
The pitch sounds like a thousand angry bees.
As I watch, it looks like a Mexican rainbow wave.
I can feel it getting close.
Then the sound washes over me like a tsunami.

James Finlay (9)
South Cave CE Primary School, Brough

Happiness

Happiness is like you have a big grin on your face.
Happiness feels like your brain is giving you strength.
When I am happy it feels like gold.
Like birds singing in the tree.
Happiness reminds me of my nanna.

Aidan Forrester (8)
Southcoates Primary School, Hull

Love

Love looks like sexy ladies
Love feels good
Love smells like strawberries
Love tastes like lipstick
When my mum and dad are together it reminds me of love
Love is the colour of red
Love sounds like two friends laughing.

Reece Brewitt (8)
Southcoates Primary School, Hull

Anger

Anger is red and purple like a red-hot fire.
Anger sounds like a large bonfire and fireworks.
It reminds me of fighting with my brother.
Like red-hot peppers dancing on your tongue.
It smells like onions and lemon juice.
It looks like flames of blue.
It feels like fire going to blow up.

Joshua Cain (8)
Southcoates Primary School, Hull

What Am I?

I run along the page
My arms fold when I close
I clap when I'm cutting
My teeth are long and sharp
My legs open and close
My nose is in the middle of my eyes.

What am I?
A: Scissors.

Abigail Rose Betts (11)
Southcoates Primary School, Hull

Love

Love looks like roses falling from the sky.
Love feels romantic.
Love tastes like strawberries in a bowl with oranges and cream.
Love smells like roses in a bed of roses.
Love reminds me of hearts falling into your eyes.
Love is the colour of pink.
Love sounds like romantic songs.

Jack Brown (7)
Southcoates Primary School, Hull

Anger

Anger is red like a pool of blood
Because of the knife that sticks in the body.
It sounds like footsteps running away.
It reminds me of the night I could hear shouting and crying.
It tastes like red-hot peppers dancing on your tongue.
It smells like squeezed big lemons in a bowl.
It looks like a ball of fire.
It feels like a fizzing rage.

Toby Hazel (9)
Southcoates Primary School, Hull

Happiness

Happiness looks like dolphins jumping
Feels like water flowing over me
Happiness tastes of oranges
Smells so fresh
Happiness sounds like dolphins
Happiness is the colour of pink
Reminds me of a holiday with dolphins.

Toni Andrews (7)
Southcoates Primary School, Hull

Fear

Fear is yellow
Fear is like a cat roaring
Fear tastes of dust
Fear roars like a screaming cat
Fear smells like polish
Fear looks like a furry mane
Fear feels soft like a teddy bear
Fear reminds me of when I first went on a roaring plane to Spain.

Chelsey Robinson (8)
Southcoates Primary School, Hull

Anger

Anger is reddish-purple like paint thrown across a piece of paper.
Anger sounds like sirens blaring at you.
Anger reminds me of fighting with my sister.
It tastes like red-hot peppers dancing on your tongue.
It smells like freshly squeezed lemons.
It looks like fire in your eyes.
It feels like a fire in my tummy.

Shanice Bell (7)
Southcoates Primary School, Hull

Anger

Anger is red and purple like an exploding bomb.
It sounds like banging and yelling.
It reminds me of Bonfire Night.
It's like red-hot peppers dancing on your tongue.

Luke Christensen (9)
Southcoates Primary School, Hull

Love

Love is pink from the petals on the ground fallen off a rose.
Love sounds like a sloppy kiss.
Love looks like the bright sun shining on me.
Love feels like a heart dying for love.
Love tastes like a lovely plate of jelly.
Love smells like a gorgeous smelling perfume.
Love reminds me of my old boyfriend.

Jessica Morgan (8)
Southcoates Primary School, Hull

Love

Love is yellow like bright sunflowers.
Love is a sound like a beautiful kiss.
Love looks like a soft kiss.
Love feels like a romantic heartbeat.
Love tastes like lovely melted chocolate.
Love smells like beautiful flowers.
Love reminds me of my teachers.

Cane Donkin (9)
Southcoates Primary School, Hull

Fear

Fear is yellow
Like cats miaowing
Tastes horrible like mud
Smells like hot crackling fire
It looks round and bumpy like a hedgehog
It feels squidgy like a balloon
Reminds me of Bonfire Night.

Megan Seaton (8)
Southcoates Primary School, Hull

Love

Love is like pink soft petals on a rose.
Love sounds like wonderful kisses.
Love looks like a romantic meal with hugs and kisses.
Love feels like a romantic heart that is full of love.
Love tastes like a wonderful plate full of melted chocolate.
Love smells like wonderful romantic kisses.
Love reminds me of my uncle's wedding.

Chloe Jackson (8)
Southcoates Primary School, Hull

Sister

Her heart is an engine.
Her eyes are headlights.
Her breath is an exhaust.
Her hair is the roof.
Her legs are wheels.
Her ears are wing mirrors.
Her clothes are the paint job.

Elliott Hepworth (10)
Southcoates Primary School, Hull

My Sister

My sister's eyes are as bright as headlights,
Her lips are as red as blood,
Her hair is as dark as a mine,
She is as tall as a skyscraper.

Kieron Cawkwell (10)
Southcoates Primary School, Hull

Dad

His hair is spaghetti.
His voice is thunder.
His eyes are headlights.
His glasses are huge mugs.
He is as tall as a wardrobe.
His ears are wings.
His teeth are the end of a knife.
His belly is jelly.
His nose is a branch off a tree.

Lauren Leigh Allison-Beedle (10)
Southcoates Primary School, Hull

Anger

Anger is clenching his fists,
Stomping and stamping round the fire.
He is charging into war,
Looking through the broken window.
He is going to kill everyone
And everything in his path.

Lara Osborne (10)
Southcoates Primary School, Hull

Scissors

I do star jumps.
I've got two big eyes.
I come in all different sizes.
I eat through paper.
I come in different colours.
I am fat or skinny.

Sasha Gabriel (11)
Southcoates Primary School, Hull

My Little Brother

My brother's eyes are sparkling headlights,
My brother's mouth is a loud radio,
My brother's nose is a ski slope,
My brother's ears are two microphones,
My brother's hair is a shiny mirror,
My brother's arms and legs are rag dolls,
My brother's eyelashes are black bristles,
My brother's fingers are vacuum cleaners,
My brother knows everything!

Kellie Adamson (10)
Southcoates Primary School, Hull

The Earring

I watch her shine and sparkle
She is in my ear
She can be small or big
Round or square
Looped or a stud
I take her out on a night
And put her in my jewellery box.

Deanna May Hughes (10)
Southcoates Primary School, Hull

Love

Love is pink like a sweet-smelling rose.
Love tastes like sweets floating in the bright sun.
Love sounds like roses singing in the back garden.
Love smells like a beautiful friend.
Love looks like a love heart shape.
Love feels like beautiful bells ringing.
Love reminds me of puppies at Christmas.

Ellie-May Betts (8)
Southcoates Primary School, Hull

Happiness

Happiness is orange like an orange ball kicked high in the sky.
Happiness tastes like red juicy strawberries.
Happiness sounds like music playing.
Happiness smells like Sunday dinner.
Happiness looks like holiday adverts on TV.
Happiness feels like strawberries dipped in cream.
Happiness reminds me of my friends, family and pets.

Ellie Winstanley (7)
Southcoates Primary School, Hull

Happiness

Happiness is green like a summer sky in the morning.
Happiness feels like fireworks at a wedding.
Happiness looks like a beautiful sunset.
Happiness sounds like wedding bells.
Happiness smells like a lovely cake baking.
Happiness tastes like the cherries dropping from the trees.
Happiness reminds me of my dad's birthday.

Amy Watkin (8)
Southcoates Primary School, Hull

Love

Love is like a red dot splashed on a piece of paper.
Love reminds me of a rose.
Love looks like a jam tart.
Love sounds like a heart pumping.
Love tastes like a Jelly Tot.
Love feels like a heart beating.
Love smells like perfume.

Tiffany Gabriel (8)
Southcoates Primary School, Hull

Happiness

Happiness is yellow like the bright summer sunshine.
Happiness tastes like fruit and veg.
Happiness sounds like birds singing from up in the trees.
Happiness smells like beautiful roses.
Happiness feels like ripe cherries.
Happiness looks like brown, furry squirrels in the trees.
Happiness reminds me of summer.

Jordan Bartley (8)
Southcoates Primary School, Hull

Love

Love is pink like a fabulous rose.
Love sounds like smooth music on a sandy beach.
Love smells like fresh lavender.
Love tastes like a strawberry dream cake covered with sugar.
Love feels like a pink quilt covered in smooth sloppy cream.
Love reminds me of Christmas Day when I sit with my family.

Lucy Betts (8)
Southcoates Primary School, Hull

Love

Love is pink like my pink rag doll.
Love smells like pink Lacoste perfume.
Love sounds like my family singing goodnight.
Love looks like someone getting married.
Love feels like me dancing in romance.
Love reminds me of the day I was born.

Libbie Thompson (8)
Southcoates Primary School, Hull

Fear

Fear is like a sheet of ice
Fear is silent
It smells like a cold foggy day
It looks like a rainy day
It feels like a miserable rainy day
It reminds me of cold days
It reminds me of scary films.

Jessica Wilkinson (8)
Southcoates Primary School, Hull

Happiness

Happiness is pink like a light pink flower.
It smells like lavender.
It feels like fluffy, bubbly clouds floating in the air.
It sounds like a child playing in the park
And it reminds me of Christmas Day.

Kallum Robins (8)
Southcoates Primary School, Hull

Love

Love is like a bright purple flower.
It smells like perfume and lavender.
It sounds like birds singing.
It tastes like a nice ice-pop on a nice sunny day.
It reminds me of a bright purple flower.

Amy Kirkwood (8)
Southcoates Primary School, Hull

Love

Love is red like a rose in the summertime.
Love sounds like roses waving from side to side.
Love smells like strawberries.
Love looks like a red marble on the ground.
Love feels like a relaxing, swishing sea.
Love reminds me of calm, quiet, relaxing, wavy wind swishing from side to side.
Love tastes like strawberries.

Sophie Walker (8)
Southcoates Primary School, Hull

Anger

Anger is red like an exploding rocket.
Anger is like a dragon blowing fire out of his mouth.
Anger feels like hot water that is burning.
Anger tastes like a strong hot chilli that is in your mouth.
Anger smells like a tomato exploding.
Anger looks like a dragon.
Anger reminds me of a volcano exploding.

Alice Watkin (8)
Southcoates Primary School, Hull

Anger

Anger is bright red like a red bouncy ball.
Anger sounds like crashing thunder.
Anger tastes like red-hot pepper.
Anger looks like a red fierce dragon.
Anger feels like a red cactus.
Anger smells like red peppers.
Anger reminds me of a hurricane.

Jack Walsh (7)
Southcoates Primary School, Hull

Love

Love is red like a red bouncy ball bouncing up and down.
It looks like a red heart on a piece of ice floating away.
It smells like beautiful perfume on a beautiful woman.
It feels like something red breaking your heart.
It sounds like a voice in your heart saying 'I love you'.
It tastes like a lovely red lollipop.
It reminds me of walking along a lovely beach on a lovely day.

Sophie Arnold (8)
Southcoates Primary School, Hull

Anger

Anger is red like hot molten lava.
Anger sounds like an earthquake high up in the mountains.
Anger looks like a devil in Hell.
Anger feels like a porcupine.
Anger smells like smoke from a volcano.
Anger tastes like a red-hot pepper.
Anger reminds me of a fierce dragon.

Callum Barton (8)
Southcoates Primary School, Hull

Anger

Anger is red like burning fire exploding.
Anger tastes like a big hot chilli.
Anger sounds like a baby screaming.
Anger smells like a tomato exploding.
Anger looks like a big dragon that is mad.
Anger feels like hot water that is burning.
Anger reminds me of someone who is fighting.

Courtney Young (8)
Southcoates Primary School, Hull

Anger

Anger is black like a shadow.
Anger tastes like pigs' kidneys.
Anger sounds like a broken violin playing the most horrible tune
in the galaxy.
Anger smells like donkey dung.
Anger looks like a devil in Hell.
Anger reminds me of evil taking over the Earth.

Joshua Martin (9)
Southcoates Primary School, Hull

Happiness

Happiness is yellow like the flaming-hot sun.
Happiness tastes like chocolate in the sweet shop.
Happiness sounds like an opera singer on the stage.
Happiness smells like an army of flowers.
Happiness looks like an angel in the sky.
Happiness feels like a teddy bear on your bed.
Happiness reminds me of people having fun all day.

Cameron Cook (9)
Southcoates Primary School, Hull

The Strange Zoo

Hyenas swim in the air
Worms eat birds
Flies eat frogs
Sheep are made out of toilet roll
Cows say miaow
Zebras eat cat food
Hippos ice skate
Hyenas go on dates with emus.

Lee Bonner (10)
Southcoates Primary School, Hull

The Strange School

We don't go to school to learn, we sit around all day.
We teach the teacher.
When it is SATs, we tell them the answers.
There are no rules because we are fools.
When they read they look at pictures instead.
When they work, they smirk all day long.
Sheep fly around the dark blue sky.
When it comes to dinner, people run round the classroom.

Charlotte Blackburn (10)
Southcoates Primary School, Hull

Anger Is . . .

A nasty swear word
A moody storm
A big, heavy breath
It's as violent as a lion
An upsetting argument
A big, vicious shout
A sulky mood
Horrid faces
Everything destroyed!

Ellie Kerins (11)
Southcoates Primary School, Hull

TV

My mum's a TV,
Helps you forget,
Always there for you,
Never stops,
Always working hard.

Sean Boddy (11)
Southcoates Primary School, Hull

What Is . . .?

What is sun?

Sun is a star
Dancing across the sky.
Sun is a rose
Dying down at sunset.

Sun is an angel
Playing hide-and-seek.
Sun is a yellow spot
Floating in the sky.

What is fog?

Fog is fire breath
Floating in the sky.
Fog is dragon smoke
Dancing in the sky.

Fog is smoke
From a giant's cooker.
Fog is a cloud of smoke
From a giant's kettle.

Lucy Edwards (9)
Southcoates Primary School, Hull

What Am I?

I am sly and sneaky,
I am horrifying and unexpected,
I am a thief taking people's souls,
My execution is fierce and evil,
I am as quick as a wolf hunting my prey,
I am as mysterious as a bloodsucking bat,
I creep up on people during the night; the young and the old,
Some people may call me the stalker,
I am a threat to the innocent and the guilty,
My hunger is still unsatisfied,
I am death.

Reece Cockerline (11)
Southcoates Primary School, Hull

What Is . . . ?

What is rain?

Rain is popping balloons
Falling from the sky.
Rain is party poppers
Being set off.
Rain is Irish dancing
Being performed.

What is sun?

The sun is a burning ring of fire
Burning into the day.
The sun is hot gas
Powering a hot air balloon.
The sun is like a giant's light bulb
Lighting up the sky.
The sun is like a circle of gold paper
Stuck onto light blue paper.

Scott Baker (9)
Southcoates Primary School, Hull

The Strange Zoo

It's raining tigers and turtles.
Lions feed the humans.
Elephants and monkeys play poker.
It is as hot as an ice block.
Giraffes and hippos get the job of zookeeper
Humans biting and kill sharks
The sky is the shape of a rhino
Leopards racing cheetahs.

Reece Stewart (10)
Southcoates Primary School, Hull

Rain Is . . . ?

Rain is . . . ?

Rain is a tap dancer
Tapping on the floor.

Rain is cats and dogs
Falling from the sky.

Sun is . . . ?

Sun is a bright button
Floating around the sky.

It is a blazing ball
Flowing in the sky.

Wind is . . . ?

Wind is a howling wolf
Howling in the woods.

It is a volcano exploding,
Red fire pouring out.

Jason Weightman (10)
Southcoates Primary School, Hull

Stars

Staring down from the night sky,
I entertain the solar system by floating around
And doing star jumps,
My glimmering skin and my joyful smile will cheer you up
And make you laugh,
And when you are waking up to start your day
I am taking my rest and fading away.

Jakob Sheffield (10)
Southcoates Primary School, Hull

What Is Rain? What Is Sun?

What is rain?
Rain is seawater
Drifting from the sky.
Rain is bubbles
Popping on the floor.
Rain is a tap
Dripping and dripping.

What is sun?
Sun is a blazing ball
Shining from the sky.
Sun is a light bulb
Hanging from the ceiling.
Sun is a sunflower
In blue water.

Rosie Plews (10)
Southcoates Primary School, Hull

A Strange Day

A strange day it was; snowing butter and bread
As cold as an ice cube
Then suddenly it was raining people and aliens

As cold as the summer air
As hot as winter snow
In houses ice cream was melting
Elephants were dancing on ice

Monkeys playing poker
Giraffes pick-pocketing old grannies
Hippos getting jobs
In the land of Moulting.

Andrew Wallace (10)
Southcoates Primary School, Hull

Weather

What is wind?

Wind is a howling wolf
Screaming out at midnight.
It is a man blowing,
Waking up the trees from their night rest.

Wind is leaves dancing
Down from their branches.
It is a fan
Drying clothes on a washing line.

What is rain?

Rain is like a balloon
Exploding in puddles.
It is drips of petrol
Leaking from an exhaust pipe.

Rain is like dogs' saliva
Pouring from their cheeks.
It is the sound of a drum
Playing in a band.

Charles Weaver (9)
Southcoates Primary School, Hull

My Mum

My mum's a teddy,
She's always warm,
Soft and cuddly,
Squishy as a lilo,
Always there.

Shannan Warelow (10)
Southcoates Primary School, Hull

What Is Rain And What Is Fog?

What is rain?
Rain is like white paint
Tapping on the windowpane.
Rain is a sheet of paper
Splashing in the puddles.
Rain is like white washing-up powder
Scattered over the city.

What is fog?
Fog is steam
From a giant's kettle
Pouring over the city.
Fog is candyfloss clouds
Falling from the sky.
Fog is breath
From a dragon's nostrils
When it's breathing.
Fog is smoke
From a burning fire.

Chloe Snell (10)
Southcoates Primary School, Hull

The Strange Portal

It was glowing boxes.
It was spitting paper aeroplanes out.
It was as cold as the sun.
It was as evil as a good Samaritan.
It was as thick as paper.
It was made of plastic.
Darth Vader came out on a flying cow
Battling Luke Skywalker on a flying elephant.

Scott Thornley (11)
Southcoates Primary School, Hull

Plants

Plants dance in the wind
Plants eat while they rub their feet
Their petals fly and their leaves wave bye
The stem walks while they talk
They make food for animals
And they can be sad and blue like you
They can times themselves and climb up garden walls
When they're asleep they snore
And when they're awake they roar
Some plants sing but others may sting
They can make their own drink
And they stink
They love knocking at the door
And can be used to clean the floor.

Selina Johnson (11)
Southcoates Primary School, Hull

Anger Is . . .

Getting as red as a rose,
Being a heavy-breathing bear,
Exploding like a bomb,
Being a violent cat,
Getting hot like fire
Destroying everything in its path,
Lashing out at everyone,
Scrunching its face up like a wrinkly dog,
Throwing a temper like a big baby,
Making a big rabble: swearing, shouting and screaming.

Amy Brown (11)
Southcoates Primary School, Hull

The Strange School

Children are teaching teachers.
We go to school to learn but do not do anything.
It says no pets allowed, but there are wild animals running around.
The girls go in the boys' toilets and the boys go in the girls'.
Boys have their hair in ponytails,
Girls wear boys' uniforms.
Boys wear girls' uniforms.
Girls spike their hair,
Boys wear make-up.
Girls wear Total 90s,
Boys wear dolly shoes.

Shauna Denman (10)
Southcoates Primary School, Hull

Anger

Suicide with a scream
Crush, kill, run
Killing comes to me.

Screaming and killing people
Bullying is good
Killing comes to me.

Crash, kill, snap
Overwhelming, shouting loud
Killing comes to me.

Shoot, fume, thrash
Scream, suicide, bully
Snap, kill, smash
Killing comes to me!

Charley Hornshaw (10)
Southcoates Primary School, Hull

What Is . . .?

What is wind?
Wind is a wolf.
Wind is a fox
Scuffling in the wind.

What is the sun?
Sun is a coin
Flying in the air.
Sun is a big orange
Floating in the sky.

What is fog?
Fog is steam
Coming from a kettle.
Fog is air
Coming from a lion's nostrils.

Charlie Bailey (10)
Southcoates Primary School, Hull

What Is . . .?

What is wind?
Wind is a wolf
Howling in the dark.
Wind is an owl
Whistling in the tree.
Wind is a cheetah
Running so fast in the jungle.

What is sun?
Sun is a bright light bulb
Shining in the sky.
Sun is a coin
Flying in a bright, pale, blue sky.

Rona Carmena Spiteri (10)
Southcoates Primary School, Hull

What Is . . . ?

What is rain?
Rain is water from a hosepipe
Sprinkling from the sky.
Rain is blue sea
Coming in drops at a time.

What is sun?
Sun is a light bulb
Shining from the sky.
Sun is a ball of fire
Watching us.

Maisie Hopkin (9)
Southcoates Primary School, Hull

What Is Red?

What is red?
A rose is red
As red as a ruby
Growing sweetly outside.

What is green?
Grass is green
As green as an emerald
Glowing in the dark.

What is yellow?
The sun is yellow
Shining like a light
As bright as a laser.

What is orange?
An orange is orange
Waiting to be eaten
Or beaten.

Louis Dearing (8)
Spring Cottage Primary School, Hull

What Is Red?

What is red?
A strawberry is red
As red as roses
And smelling so sweet and juicy.

What is purple?
A plum is purple
As purple as purple grapes
Sitting in the fruit bowl waiting to be eaten.

What is pink?
A pig is pink
As pink as a tongue
Sitting in the glowing sun.

What is blue?
The sky is blue
As blue as a sapphire
With white fluffy clouds all over.

What is yellow?
A banana is yellow
Smelling as sweet as honey
Hanging on a tree.

Shelby Swaby (9)
Spring Cottage Primary School, Hull

What Is Green?

What is green?
A pear is green
Soft and juicy
Or hard and crunchy.

What is yellow?
The sun is yellow
Just so hot
Gloaming in the air.

What is orange?
A pumpkin is orange
Scaring children
At Hallowe'en.

What is red?
A ruby is red
Shining brightly
In your eyes.

What is blue?
A blueberry is blue
Just so juicy
Good to eat.

George Thompson (9)
Spring Cottage Primary School, Hull

What Is Red?

What is red?
Lipstick is red
Strawberries are red
As red as a ruby.

What is pink?
A cherry is pink
Shining in the fruit bowl.

What is yellow?
The sun is yellow
Glowing in the blue sky
Twinkling like a star.

What is green?
The grass is green
Cut short in the garden.

What is purple?
A plum is purple
Juicy and ready to eat.

Natasha Richardson (8)
Spring Cottage Primary School, Hull

What Is Red?

What is red?
A poppy is red
Gleaming and growing
And spreading that lovely smell.

What is green?
A frog is green
Leaping in the water.

What is yellow?
The sun is yellow
Throwing heat to us.

What is orange?
Oranges are orange
Sat in a fruit bowl waiting
To be eaten.

What is blue?
The sky is blue
Just like a sapphire.

Sarah Jordan (8)
Spring Cottage Primary School, Hull

What Is Yellow?

What is yellow?
A daffodil is yellow,
Sat in my garden,
Looking bright and happy.

What is yellow?
Sunshine is yellow,
Shining sweetly
In the sky.

What is yellow?
A melon is yellow,
Waiting patiently in the supermarket
To be bought.

What is yellow?
A Smartie is yellow,
Sitting patiently in its tube,
Sitting there waiting to be let out.

Emma Hewison (8)
Spring Cottage Primary School, Hull

What Is Red?

What is red?
A poppy is red
Waiting to be picked
In the sunlight.

What is green?
An emerald is green
In my garden
Beneath the rocks.

What is purple?
Ribena is purple
A special drink
So tempting to drink a sip.

What is blue?
A bluebell is blue
Dying to be watered
So bad its soil is drying up.

Ryan Rhoades (8)
Spring Cottage Primary School, Hull

What Is Blue?

What is blue?
A sapphire is blue,
Gleaming in every direction
In the sun!

What is green?
Grass is green,
Green as an emerald
Growing in my back garden.

What is yellow?
A banana is yellow
As rich as gold
In a fruit bowl.

What is red?
An apple is red,
As red as a ruby,
The shiniest on a tree.

What is orange?
An orange is orange
As mouth-watering
As can be!

Sophie Louise Maw (8)
Spring Cottage Primary School, Hull

What Is Red?

What is red?
A strawberry is red
As red as a ruby
And tasting so juicy.

What is green?
Grapes are green
As green as grass
And tasting so delicious

What is blue?
The sea is blue
As blue as the sky
With ships floating across the ocean.

What is yellow?
A banana is yellow
Hanging in a tree
Waiting to be picked.

What is orange?
A tangerine is orange
As orange as Mars
Looking so juicy!

Jack Edward Dawson (9)
Spring Cottage Primary School, Hull

What Is Red?

What is red?
A strawberry is red
As red as a ruby
And looking so juicy.

What is red?
A cherry is red
As red as blood
And looking so ripe.

What is red?
A poppy is red
As red as strawberry juice
Smelling so fresh.

What is red?
A tomato is red
As red as red pen
Looking so bright.

Eleanor Tyas (9)
Spring Cottage Primary School, Hull

What Is Red?

What is red?
A ruby is red
As red as red can be
Lying in a jewel shop.

What is green?
A frog is green
Hopping on a lily pad
In the shiny pond

What is yellow?
Butter is yellow
Spreading on bread
From the jar.

What is blue?
The sky is blue
Taller than a skyscraper
With the clouds.

Lloyd Gurnell (9)
Spring Cottage Primary School, Hull

What Is Pink?

What is pink
Nail varnish is pink
As sparkly as glitter
Sparkling in the night!

What is red?
Strawberries are red
As red as rubies
Juicy and sweet!

What is yellow?
The sun is yellow
Gleaming in the sky
Like a twinkle in my eye.

What is blue?
The ocean is blue
Sparkling and twinkling
Everywhere!

What is orange?
Carrots are orange
Ripe and crunchy
And ready to eat!

Courtney Rose Meakes (8)
Spring Cottage Primary School, Hull

What Is Yellow?

What is yellow?
The sun is yellow
As hot as fire
Burning in the town.

What is red?
Strawberries are red
On a small bush
Waiting to bo picked.

What is blue?
The sea is blue
As blue as the sky
Washing things up onto the shore.

What is purple?
Grapes are purple
In the fruit bowl
Waiting to be eaten.

What is green?
Cucumber is green
In the cold fridge
Looking yummy.

Ashleigh Dixon
Spring Cottage Primary School, Hull

What Is Red?

What is red?
A rose is red
Smelling so sweet
As red as a ruby.

What is white?
A sheep is white
Wagging its tail
In the sunlight.

What is green?
A leaf is green
Floating gently
In the air.

What is yellow?
A banana is yellow
Sitting in a bowl
Waiting to be peeled.

Ellie Johnson (8)
Spring Cottage Primary School, Hull

Young Writers Information

We hope you have enjoyed reading this book - and that you will continue to enjoy it in the coming years.

If you like reading and writing poetry drop us a line, or give us a call, and we'll send you a free information pack.

Alternatively if you would like to order further copies of this book or any of our other titles, then please give us a call or log onto our website at
www.youngwriters.co.uk

Young Writers Information
Remus House
Coltsfoot Drive
Peterborough
PE2 9JX

(01733) 890066